The Teutonic Knights

A Captivating Guide to a Catholic Military Order and Their Role in the Crusades and Impact in Europe during the Middle Ages

© Copyright 2021

All Rights Reserved. No part of this book may be reproduced in any form without permission in writing from the author. Reviewers may quote brief passages in reviews.

Disclaimer: No part of this publication may be reproduced or transmitted in any form or by any means, mechanical or electronic, including photocopying or recording, or by any information storage and retrieval system, or transmitted by email without permission in writing from the publisher.

While all attempts have been made to verify the information provided in this publication, neither the author nor the publisher assumes any responsibility for errors, omissions or contrary interpretations of the subject matter herein.

This book is for entertainment purposes only. The views expressed are those of the author alone, and should not be taken as expert instruction or commands. The reader is responsible for his or her own actions.

Adherence to all applicable laws and regulations, including international, federal, state and local laws governing professional licensing, business practices, advertising and all other aspects of doing business in the US, Canada, UK or any other jurisdiction is the sole responsibility of the purchaser or reader.

Neither the author nor the publisher assumes any responsibility or liability whatsoever on the behalf of the purchaser or reader of these materials. Any perceived slight of any individual or organization is purely unintentional.

Free Bonus from Captivating History (Available for a Limited time)

Hi History Lovers!

Now you have a chance to join our exclusive history list so you can get your first history ebook for free as well as discounts and a potential to get more history books for free! Simply visit the link below to join.

Captivatinghistory.com/ebook

Also, make sure to follow us on Facebook, Twitter and Youtube by searching for Captivating History.

Contents

INTRODUCTION: CRUSADERS WITH A SIDE HUSTLE?.............. 1
CHAPTER 1 - THE TEUTONIC KNIGHTS ARRIVE IN EASTERN EUROPE 5
CHAPTER 2 - FIGHTING FOR THEIR VERY SURVIVAL...............14
CHAPTER 3 - TAKING ON LITHUANIA 23
CHAPTER 4 - STRUGGLING TO HANG ON 34
CHAPTER 5 - THE PEACE OF THORN AND ITS AFTERMATH 44
CHAPTER 6 - THE STAGE IS SET..50
CHAPTER 7 - STANDING AT THE PRECIPICE 58
CHAPTER 8 - ON A TIDAL WAVE OF TEUTONIC REFORMATION 67
CHAPTER 9 - ON BATTLEFIELDS FAR AND WIDE.......................75
CHAPTER 10 - THE LATER YEARS OF THE TEUTONIC ORDER..81
CONCLUSION: FROM THE CRUSADES TO HUMANITARIAN AID 87
HERE'S ANOTHER BOOK BY CAPTIVATING HISTORY THAT YOU MIGHT LIKE 90
FREE BONUS FROM CAPTIVATING HISTORY (AVAILABLE FOR A LIMITED TIME) 91

Introduction: Crusaders with a Side Hustle?

"If you are an Arabic-speaking Greek-Orthodox going to a French school it makes you deeply skeptical if you have to listen to three different accounts of the Crusades—one from the Muslim side, one from the Greek side, and one from the Catholic side."

-Nassim Nicholas Taleb

In many ways, the order of crusading knights known as the Teutonic Knights has been largely misunderstood—perhaps even more misunderstood (if such a thing is possible) than the Crusades themselves. For one thing, since the Teutonic Knights are German in origin, many have falsely equated the Teutonic Order with the German nationalism that arose in the 20th century. For those who see similarities, however, it is always an inconvenient truth to point out that when Hitler took over Austria, one of the first things he did was disband the last vestiges of the Teutonic Order!

It is true that the Nazis used the imagery of conquering the Teutonic Knights in their own propaganda as a means to try and legitimatize the taking of land previously controlled by them. But if the Nazis really were such big fans of the Teutonic Order, it seems rather strange that they were the ones who got rid of it. It is also rather inconvenient to such a narrative, as the German nationalism that existed in the 20th century was not present during much of the history of the Teutonic Knights. Modern-day Germany, in fact, did not exist for much of the knights' history.

Germany as a nation state did not come into being until 1871. Prior to this, what we now call Germany was a part of various amalgamations of Western and Central European confederations, such as the Holy Roman Empire, Austria-Hungary, and Prussia. It is true that the Teutonic Knights were made up of Teutons, the Latin term for Germans in general, but that is not much different than the fact that the Knights Templar were primarily French.

The Teutonic Knights could be known as the "other Crusaders" or perhaps even the Crusaders with a side mission. Because, unlike their peers, the Knights Hospitaller and the Knights Templar, who were primarily famous for waging war against the powers of Islam, the Teutonic Knights were given a crusade of another kind. They were sent to do battle with the pagans of Europe.

However, the Teutonic Knights began their ministry not as a fighting force but as caretakers of the sick. Their origins actually stem all the way back to 1118 when the Hospital of Saint Mary of the Germans was established in the city of Jerusalem. This was not a military base or fortress but, just as the title implies, a hospital to tend to the sick. This hospital specialized in caring for German-speaking visitors to the Holy Land and was partially overseen and protected by the Knights Hospitaller.

The Crusaders lost Jerusalem to invading Muslim armies in 1187, and the Hospital of Saint Mary of the Germans in Jerusalem ceased to exist. Now fast forward a few years later to 1190 in the Crusader outpost of Acre, some eighty miles north of the fallen Jerusalem. At this place and time, German volunteers established a new field hospital for the sick and injured. In homage to the previous German-run hospital in Jerusalem, this new treatment center was also given the name of Hospital of Saint Mary.

The hospital became well known for its selfless efforts to tend to the sick and injured. Holy Roman Emperor Henry VI soon took a keen interest in this German presence at Acre and sponsored the establishment of a German military order patterned after the Knights Hospitaller and Knights Templar. Initially, the early Teutonic Knights were the "medic" of the crusading forces, but their roles were quickly expanded to include fighting on the front lines.

The first grand master of the Teutonic Knights was a well-connected noble from the German region of Thuringia—Hermann von Salza. Hermann von Salza was involved in operations in the Holy Land since at least 1198, and he had subsequently proved his mettle in the Fifth Crusade, which was launched in 1217. Although the Fifth Crusade was largely a failure that resulted in a truce, Hermann von Salza had indeed proven himself to be an able commander.

Hermann von Salza also had a close relationship with Emperor Henry VI's son, Frederick II. And when Frederick II ascended to the throne of the Holy Roman Empire in 1220, he started to actively work with the Teutonic Order. Frederick began to regard the Teutonic Knights as the main representatives of the Holy Roman Empire's military might in the Holy Land.

Although the new military order was now shouldering a combat role as well as tending to the injured, Pope Gregory IX still found it prudent to recommend that the Knights Hospitaller take a leadership role over the new order. In this new arrangement, tensions between the orders were commonplace. And as the new kids on the block, the Teutonic Knights often rubbed members of the older military orders the wrong way, so much so that in 1241, the Knights Templar and the Teutonic Knights actually engaged in a skirmish with one another.

As mentioned, when the Teutonic Order was made official, the Crusader kingdom had been reduced to little more than a toehold in the city of Acre. The First Crusade called in 1090 by Pope Urban II to defend Christian pilgrims and to stave off Muslim incursions against the Byzantine Empire had been a smashing success. But by the time the Teutonic Knights came into their own, Jerusalem was lost, and the Crusaders had nearly been driven out of the region, with only a much smaller base of operations in the northwestern Levant.

At any rate, the Teutonic Knights, after being commissioned by the pope, were on the front lines of Acre, tending to the sick and wounded. The Teutonic Knights had another interesting task as well in the form of running the main ports of Acre. These ports controlled shipping from Europe to this lonely Crusader outpost, and the Teutonic Knights exacted fees from all who used the ports. This meant that pilgrims on their way to pay homage to holy sites, as well as merchants sailing across the Mediterranean to conduct trade, would have added some worth to the Teutonic coffers. Most people would have paid without much complaint since the expenditure was thought to be worth it, as the armed Crusaders provided them with valuable protection and security. The Middle East was a dangerous place after all, and one could never be too careful.

At any rate, the Teutonic Knights would build up much of its early revenue from these fees. But with the Crusader kingdom being constantly squeezed by hostile forces, the future for this Crusader foothold in the Holy Land continued to look bleak. Stuck in a seemingly intractable quagmire, many a good knight began to look toward secondary missions outside of the region.

In the meantime, a large contingent of Teutonic Knights would find some rather promising prospects elsewhere. They found a new home in Eastern Europe and were soon given a new task. They would no longer battle Muslims in faraway lands but rather infidels and heretics who were much closer to home.

The Teutonic Knights would establish outposts in the wild fringes of civilization right in the backyard of the pagan strongholds of Eastern Europe. Although the Holy Land would remain a primary focus of Crusaders for many more years to come, upon their arrival in the Balkans and then ultimately the Baltic, the Teutonic Knights opened up a whole new crusading front.

Chapter 1 – The Teutonic Knights Arrive in Eastern Europe

"The surest way to work up a crusade in favor of some good cause is to promise people they will have a chance of maltreating someone. To be able to destroy with good conscience, to be able to behave badly and call your bad behavior 'righteous indignation'—this is the height of psychological luxury, the most delicious of moral treats."

-Aldous Huxley

At the dawning of the 13th century, due to the seismic shifts taking place in the Holy Land, the Teutonic Knights were in need of redeployment. The next best opportunity for the budding order came when the king of Hungary, Andrew II, requested the aid of an able fighting force in the Balkan frontiers of Transylvania in Eastern Europe. Yes, the land that Vlad III (better known as Vlad the Impaler) would later make famous was caught in a terrible struggle between the forces of Hungary and the Cumans, a Turkic nomadic people that had been making inroads in the region.

This was not the first time that German forces were sent to aid a king of Hungary. In 1060, Hungarian King Solomon was actually kicked off the throne by his uncle Béla. The German knights made sure that he was restored in 1063. Even prior to the founding of the Teutonic Order, German soldiers from the Germanic-based Holy Roman Empire were already deeply involved with the affairs of Eastern Europe.

This most recent request by a Hungarian king coincided with the elevation of a formidable grand master of the Teutonic Order— Hermann von Salza. King Andrew II had granted Hermann von Salza's knights' territory in the region right between Transylvania and Wallachia, known as the Burzenland. It was here that the knights built a lonely outpost on top of a rocky outcropping. This fortress would become known as Bran Castle. Bran Castle is famous for becoming the home of the aforementioned Vlad III, adding even more legend and mystique to this shadowy time and place in history. This citadel was just one of several that the knights had erected in the region.

It was here in the borderlands of Wallachia and Transylvania that the knights perfected their hallmark strategy of conducting lightning raids and then rushing back to the safety of their fortresses when the odds turned against them. At any rate, the Teutonic Knights were successful in pushing back the Cumans, but as far as the king of Hungary was concerned, the victorious Teutonic Knights began to get just a little bit too comfortable.

And once it seemed that they were trying to set up their own base of operations in Transylvania, Andrew II rose up against them. However, the Teutonic Knights did not just create this foothold of their own accord; they actually had the backing of Pope Honorius III. King Andrew II had also previously promised the knights land and even tax breaks in exchange for their services. The Teutonic Knights were then able to build up several strong fortresses and even encourage other Germans to settle in the region.

Yet all of that seemed to have been forgotten. And by 1225, King Andrew II, frustrated with Teutonic encroachment on royal lands, as well as the fact that the order had begun to mint its own coins, began to grow wary of this foreign armed encampment on Transylvanian soil. He rallied his own homegrown troops and forced the knights to leave. The Teutonic Knights were now once again without a castle in which they could hang their helmet.

Soon enough, however, international intrigue in Eastern Europe would provide them with new territory to lay claim to. Poland had been trying to convert the pagans of Prussia by force. Prussia, of course, is a nation state in Eastern Europe that no longer exists. But in those days, it made up a region that roughly corresponded with the southeastern shores of the Baltic. Polish King Boleslaw IV had tried to subdue the pagans in 1173, but much of these efforts died with him when he perished that very year.

More inroads against the pagans were made in the early 13th century. Once the first Prussian bishop was appointed in 1215, he received the backing of Polish Duke Conrad of Mazovia. But the loose confederation of Prussian tribes could not be tamed by either the bishop or Conrad, and in the 1220s, pagan Prussian marauders launched several attacks against churches in the region, as well as Polish settlements in Mazovia, killing and enslaving anyone they came across.

This, of course, was more than enough reason for the Polish powers that be to want to strike back. So, with the pope's blessing, the Teutonic Knights and the forces of Duke Conrad of Mazovia waged war on the Prussians. Operations began in earnest in 1226, and the Teutonic Knights fought with a promise from the duke that new territory would come into their possession as a reward for their efforts. The pope even officially weighed in by issuing a papal bull leveled squarely against the Prussians in 1230.

Several years of conflict then kicked off, in which both sides committed acts that today would most certainly be considered war crimes. The Teutonic Knights mercilessly slaughtered any and all Prussians who refused to convert to Christianity. The pagan Prussians performed literal human sacrifices of Teutonic Knights whenever and wherever they captured them. This conflict was about as brutal as they come, with neither side giving much of any quarter to the other.

The first wave of fighting began in 1231 when a relatively small band of Teutonic Knights assembled in Prussia; they were backed up by the larger forces of Poland and Pomerelia. Since it is important to understand the lay of the land in those days for context, it must be noted that the place called Pomerelia was a subdivision of a larger region referred to as Pomerania. The whole region of Pomerania is located between modern-day Germany and modern-day Poland. Pomerelia was on the eastern side of Pomerania, where the bustling city of Danzig (now Gdansk) was located. Outside of Pomerelia, one would find themselves in the lands of the pagan Prussians.

Having said that, from here on out, it was a slow push east through the wild and unwelcoming terrain of Prussia. And as the Teutonic Knights drove out the enemy, they established fortresses on the newly conquered territory. These formidable citadels made of stone gave the Teutonic Knights a great advantage over the Prussian pagans. The native peoples of Prussia at this time were building their own fortresses out of wood, and masonry work like the Teutonic Knights was capable of was practically unknown to them. This meant that while their own forts could be easily overrun and burned to the ground, the knights could hole up in their stone castles almost indefinitely, with the Prussian warriors unable to penetrate their thick stone and brick walls. Bearing testament to just how well these fortresses were built, many still stand to this day.

Immigrants from the German homeland settled around these fortresses. In order to eliminate confusion, it is important to point out that modern-day Germany did not exist in those days. So, when we speak of the "German homeland," we are actually referring to the Holy Roman Empire. The Holy Roman Empire, which considered itself an inheritor of the fallen Western Roman Empire of old, was a conglomeration of western, central, and some eastern European lands. The Holy Roman Empire roughly encompassed all of modern-day Germany, Belgium, the Netherlands, eastern France, northern Italy, and pieces of several other states in Eastern Europe. German immigrants began to pour into Russia from the Holy Roman Empire to farm the lands surrounding the heavily fortified territory of the Teutonic Knights.

Along with farmers, important skilled workers, tradesmen, and financiers also set up shop in the newly conquered territory. This Teutonic-controlled land was referred to as the Monastic State of the Teutonic Order. With this growing German presence right on the doorstep of Poland, it was not long before Polish authorities began to feel a little uneasy.

The Polish powers that be were certainly glad that the pagan Prussians were no longer raiding their lands, but now another Christian—yet largely alien—culture was taking root. And in a virtual repeat of what had transpired in Hungary, Polish leaders began to wish that the Teutonic Knights and their hangers-on had somewhere else to gather.

Another monastic order, the Livonian Brothers of the Sword (or as they were later called the Livonian Knights), was having an increasingly difficult time against the pagan forces of neighboring Lithuania. They had previously waged war against Estonia and Latvia, which in those days was lumped together as Livonia, but the Lithuanians proved a particularly tough nut to crack.

Pagans from Lithuania had been raiding nearby Christian villages, and their pirate crafts had been preying upon merchants. Some missionary efforts had been made to convince the Lithuanians to convert, but the conversion rate was not as fast as the Vatican would have liked. As such, in 1195, Pope Celestine III launched a crusade to have the Lithuanians converted by force.

Since it was essentially a mission to force pagans to convert by way of the sword, it seemed to only make sense that the crusading knights were called the "Brothers of the Sword." At any rate, although the Livonian Brothers of the Sword were successful in the early days of their crusade in Livonia, they were having an exceedingly hard time against nearby Lithuania.

In the Battle of Saule, which took place on September 22nd, 1236, the Lithuanian fighters completely trounced the Livonian Knights after they became surrounded in the Samogitian swamplands. It was a terrible blow for the knights, in which at least sixty of their number, along with the order's own grand master—Volkwin—were killed in the melee.

In fact, the Livonian Order was so thoroughly destroyed that it was decided that the remnants would be absorbed into the Teutonic Knights. They would remain a distinct branch of the Teutonic Knights, but they would be ultimately under the charge of the Teutonic grand master. After the failure of the Livonian Brothers of the Sword, the reconstituted Teutonic Knights had to pick up where the decimated Livonian Knights had left off.

The pope gave his blessing for a renewed crusade against the Lithuanians, and the following year, the Teutonic Knights were redeployed to the front lines of Livonia. They made themselves at home in the Livonian Brothers' old domain, and the Teutonic Knights were soon calling their new base of operations "Saint Mary's Land" in homage to their origins in the Levant as the Hospital of Saint Mary.

Symbolism, you see, is powerful, and the Teutonic Knights were willing to use it to strengthen their grip on the region. They even went as far as to use rhetoric uttered in 1215 at the Fourth Lateran Council to their own ends. At this council, Pope Innocent III had proclaimed that Livonia was the "land of the Mother of God." His words obviously cannot be taken literally since Mother Mary was clearly from the Middle East, not the Baltic.

But ever since the Catholic Church had made inroads in the region, a so-called "cult of Mary" had been promoted. And it was apparently with this reverence in mind that the pope had dubbed Livonia as the "land of the Mother of God." The Teutonic Knights had since become determined to make this into a literal translation and used the notion that they were defending "Saint Mary's Land" as justification for their presence in Livonia.

If the Teutonic Order's chronicler Nikolaus von Jeroschin is to be believed, there were knights who even claimed to have had apparitions of Mary while serving in Saint Mary's Land. There are many stories of wounded knights on the battlefield being visited by the Virgin Mary and being miraculously healed of physical as well as psychological wounds (many of the brethren had acute cases of what we would call PTSD).

There can be no doubt, however, that all of this was also a great marketing ploy to make these far reaches of Eastern Europe more appealing to would-be settlers from the Germanic lands of the west. Suddenly, Livonia was not a center of paganism but the land of Mother Mary, and as such, it was quite an attractive place for Christian settlement. And as their power base grew, the Teutonic Knights began to push farther and farther east.

This eastward push soon led to the famous engagement known as the Battle on the Ice, in which the Teutonic Knights faced off against a group of Russian warriors led by a Novgorod prince by the name of Alexander Nevsky. Although these Russians were Christians, the fact that they belonged to the Eastern Orthodox faith put them at odds with the Catholic Crusaders.

Ever since the Great Schism of 1054, the official stance of the Vatican was that Orthodox Christians of the East were in error. In truth, if the Teutonic Knights could defeat these Orthodox Christians and forcefully convert them to Catholicism, church officials most likely would have approved of their efforts. The Russians were not going to be taken down easily, though. The Battle on the Ice would prove to be a spectacular defeat of the Teutonic Knights.

The fighting began on April 5th, 1242, on Lake Peipus (sometimes referred to as Lake Chud), located between Estonia and Russia, which was frozen solid ice at the time. Alexander Nevsky had been trying to lure the Crusaders out into an open fight for some time, and on April 5th, he was finally able to do so.

Meeting him out on the lake was a Crusader force of over two thousand men, approximately half of which was infantry. Of these two thousand troops, only one hundred of them were Teutonic Knights. As always, the Teutonic Knights stood as the vanguard—a kind of elite medieval force ready to pick up the slack. Indeed, the Teutonic Knights were such well-trained and efficient fighters that just one knight could easily do the part of two or even three regular soldiers.

Alexander Nevsky, on the other hand, had a force of over four thousand warriors at his disposal. Although the Crusaders were heavily outnumbered, it was believed that their advanced armor, weapons, and techniques would see them through, as had been the case countless times before. But Alexander Nevsky proved to be much more formidable than anyone had bargained for.

Once the Teutonic Knights led their army across the frozen lake, they were stopped in their tracks by a Russian infantry absolutely hellbent on pushing them back. A bloody battle ensued, replete with all of the medieval horrors of hacking, slicing, and bludgeoning. This went on for a couple of hours when Alexander Nevsky, seeing his opportunity, suddenly gave the word for the right and left flanks of his forces, which had remained behind, to surge forward to encircle the Crusaders.

The Teutonic commanders realized what was happening, and they ordered their men to pull back, but the retreat was disorderly, with troops literally falling and slipping on the ice. It was an unmitigated disaster. Even worse, as the Teutonic Knights attempted to make a hurried dash to the other side of the lake, the extra weight of their armor and their heavy footsteps proved to be enough to crack the ice. It has been said that several of them fell right through the cracking ice and perished before ever making it to the other side. However, it must be noted that some historians have since called into question whether this account of knights falling through the ice actually happened or was a later exaggeration. Whatever the case may be, the Teutonic Knights were soundly defeated by the Russians, and those that were lucky enough managed to escape and flee back to their fortified territories.

The fact that the Russians beat the Teutonic Knights would prove quite pivotal since it would make both the Teutonic Order and their backers in the Vatican think twice before trying to make any further inroads in the east. If the Teutonic Knights were so easily defeated by the Russians, it would not make much sense to risk massive resources attempting to force Russia's Orthodox Christians to become Catholic.

It also affected the overall conversion effort of pagans in the region, leading to uprisings of both native Estonians and Prussians, as they sensed the knights' weakness from their sudden reversals. The might of Orthodox Russia would prove to be the great speed bump to the Teutonic advance. From here on out, the Teutonic war machine would inevitably begin to slow down.

Chapter 2 – Fighting for Their Very Survival

"The idea that the Crusades and the fight of Christendom against Islam is somehow an aggression on our part is absolutely antihistorical. And that is what the perception is by the American Left who hates Christendom. What I'm talking about is onward American soldiers. What we're talking about are core American values."

-Rick Santorum

In the aftermath of the famous Battle on the Ice, a revolt broke out in Pomerania. Although modern readers would probably be more adept at identifying the Pomeranian dog breed than where the region of Pomerania was on the map, this territory lay between modern-day Germany and Poland.

As it pertains to the revolt of 1242, the trouble began when the Polish duke who was administering Pomerania at the time—Duke Swantopelk—struck a bargain with recent pagan converts and sought to drive out the Teutonic Knights. It seems that the duke and his supporters had grown weary of all of the German migrants who had flooded the region due to the dominance of the Teutonic Knights.

And as had been the case in Hungary, Polish nobles such as Duke Swantopelk were growing alarmed at the increasing German influence and decided to rid themselves of it by getting rid of their benefactors—the Teutonic Knights. Since the Teutonic Knights had lent Poland considerable aid in fighting its pagan enemies, to say that the Teutonic Knights felt betrayed would be an understatement.

The turncoat duke was also of considerable concern for them because he was well acquainted with the Teutonic Order and had a keen understanding of their methods of war. The duke understood that the knights liked to launch quick lightning raids from their fortresses, catching their enemies off guard. The duke sought to turn the tables on the knights by staging ambushes on the knights' own territory.

The duke never let the knights rest, as he orchestrated multiple attacks on the Teutonic Knights' home turf. The Teutonic Knights couldn't fight on perpetually, and one by one, their fortresses were defeated. By 1244, the Teutonic Knights barely had any of their original territory left under their control—it is said that all but three of their fortresses had been compromised by Prussian/Pomeranian attacks.

Duke Swantopelk then sought to box the remnants of the knights by building so-called "counter forts" of his own, surrounding the last pocket of Teutonic resistance. However, the worst was yet to come. A major assault on the Teutonic Knights occurred around the town of Rensen, in which a whole contingent of knights was defeated; two marshals—essentially deputies of the grand master—were also killed.

It looked pretty bleak for the Teutonic Knights, but they were eventually able to rally themselves and took the fight back to their attackers. Proving that they were indeed skilled in siege warfare, the knights were able to topple the fortresses of their enemies. And even the Prussian hit-and-run attacks began to falter, as was evidenced outside the settlement of Torun in 1246 when a Prussian sneak attack was deftly repulsed by the Teutonic Knights.

The resistance was then finally crushed in late 1247 when the forces of Duke Swantopelk lost the will to fight. Duke Swantopelk's fate was sealed when the political forces of the day decisively moved against him. Both the Polish nobles and the Vatican began to condemn his actions and pressured the duke to come to terms with the Teutonic Knights.

The belligerents were then forced to seek peace, which led to the signing of the so-called Treaty of Christburg in the spring of 1249. But this peace did not come without a cost for the Teutonic Knights. As part of the agreement, the knights had to promise to allow independent bishoprics (independent of Teutonic control, that is), as well as pledge to be more lenient on pagan converts to Christianity.

Perhaps the Teutonic Knights were not "lenient" enough since the situation broke down once again in 1260, leading to a renewed Prussian/pagan revolt against the Teutonic Knights. The rebellion unfolded in the aftermath of the Battle of Durbe in Latvia, in which a stunning 150 Teutonic Knights were slaughtered by an army of Samogitians and Lithuanians.

The battle took place on July 13th, 1260, after the Samogitians launched an assault on the Teutonic fortress of Georgenburg. This led to a coalition of Teutonic and Livonian Knights deciding to work with an infantry of native Prussians and Curonians. Yes, even though there was a generalized revolt against the Teutonic Knights, not all Prussians took part in it. Some remained loyal to the Teutonic Order and agreed to join them in their struggle. This multi-faceted coalition marched on Georgenburg to rescue the besieged contingent of knights. The two opposing armies converged near the Durbe River.

However, the knights were betrayed by the Curonians who made up their rearguard, and they soon found themselves being attacked on all sides. It was this deadly betrayal that led to not only the loss of 150 Teutonic Knights but also the death of Livonian Grand Master Burkhard von Hornhausen.

Not missing a chance to kick a man (or an order of knights for that matter) when he's down, this spectacular defeat encouraged the pagan Prussians of Pomerania to strike out at the knights once more. This time, the rebellion was led by a man by the name of Herkus Monte. Just like Swantopelk before him, Monte was well acquainted with the knights, and as such, he thought he had a pretty good idea of how to deal with them.

Monte, in fact, had been a prisoner of war during the previous round of fighting, so he got to see firsthand the inner workings of the brotherhood. He was little more than a child at the time, and the knights showed mercy on him, allowing him to live with them for ten years. Herkus was even educated by the knights, as he was personally tutored at one of their monasteries.

Herkus was apparently a firm believer that no good deed should go unpunished, and he would end up using all of these lessons against the knights. And as a grown man in 1261, he successfully trounced the Teutonic Knights at the Battle of Pokarwis.

In this battle, the Teutonic Knights initially faced a smaller contingent of rebels, and as such, they decided to split into two groups so that they could fan out and take on combatants who might have been positioned farther afield. Herkus Monte, who was leading a contingent of Prussians, anticipated this move. He called upon his main army to assault the remaining garrison of Teutonic Knights after the other half had broken away. They were able to easily defeat the remaining half. Herkus then sent his troops to hunt down the other portion of Teutonic Knights that had repositioned themselves, and his men easily took them out as well.

An even worse fate was in store for many of the German civilians who had come to settle the regions surrounding Teutonic fortresses. According to the famed chronicler of the Teutonic Knights, Nikolaus von Jeroschin, the average man, woman, and child were not the least bit safe during these bloody revolts. As Jeroschin tells us, "Their [German settlers'] wives and children were taken prisoner in scenes of great wretchedness and kept as slaves in perpetual captivity. It was pitiful to see these noble women who had been brought up as gentlewomen and now had to suffer such painful humiliation and were brutally forced to work. It was the worst imaginable situation for them."

This string of heavy defeats nearly caused the Teutonic Order to collapse. But as had been their habit throughout their history, they were once again able to seize victory from the jaws of defeat. The very next year, Herkus Monte was temporarily out of commission due to a terrible wound he had sustained in the Siege of Konigsberg. Pope Urban IV, in the meantime, had made a call to arms, asking the leading powers of Europe to send troops to aid the faltering Teutonic Order.

These reinforcements and subsequent Prussian losses helped to stem the tide, but ultimately, the fighting would not cease until 1283 when the last of the rebels were rooted out. Ironically enough, toward the end of the conflict, when the Prussian resistance had been reduced to little more than guerilla fighting in the wilderness, the Teutonic Knights actually employed Prussian mercenaries to do their dirty work for them. The knights were content to remain holed up in their fortresses at this point and allow well-trained Prussians, well-versed in the art of ambush, to hunt down their fellow countrymen.

Back in the Holy Land, the Crusader foothold in the Levant, centered around the city of Acre, was on its last legs. At this point, a small contingent of Teutonic Knights remained with their fellow Knights Templar and Knights Hospitaller, bravely taking a stand against increasingly insurmountable odds. One must wonder if the Crusaders weren't so distracted by the events in the Baltic, perhaps a better defense of this last Crusader bastion in the Holy Land could have been mounted?

At any rate, in 1290, the pope did his best to raise money and auxiliary troops to bolster the faltering position of the defenders of Acre. And a modest group of fighters was indeed sent from Italy in the summer of 1290. These men, who mostly hailed from Lombardy and Tuscany, were inexperienced and not too keen on military discipline. This was evidenced shortly after their arrival when the overeager mercenaries accidentally slaughtered a group of Arab traders who had come to town simply to do business.

The main Muslim powerbroker in the Levant at this time was the Egyptian-based Mamluk Empire. In 1290, the Crusaders of Acre had established an uneasy truce with the Mamluks. This embarrassing incident caused by the new troops threatened to spark an all-out war. Seeking peace, the Crusader authorities in Acre had the culprits of the massacre arrested and sent an official apology to the sultan in Egypt.

This was not quite enough, though, as the Egyptian Sultan Qalawun immediately ordered the perpetrators to be turned directly over to him. The Crusaders knew that the men were guilty of an unprovoked attack, but they also knew that handing them over to the sultan would no doubt be a fate worse than death. They could not bring themselves to subject fellow Christians to such abuse and torture.

So, upon their refusal to cave to his demands, the Egyptian sultan broke the truce and renewed hostilities against the Crusaders of Acre. The Mamluks were ready to assault the Crusaders with a vengeance, and a huge force of Muslim fighters camped just outside of Acre's walled fortifications in April of 1291.

It was now clear to all involved that they were playing a zero-sum game. If the Crusaders were to lose, the Holy Land in its entirety would be lost, and all of them would most likely be slaughtered. It was literally do or die. So, the Knights Hospitaller, Knights Templar, and the small band of Teutonic Knights that remained all joined forces and prepared to lead one last defense of this besieged city. Interestingly and dramatically enough, all three grand masters of each order were actually present during this climactic struggle.

Mamluk siege engines began to slam into the fortifications on April 6th, and their engineers tried their best to dig underneath the structures in an attempt to cause the walls to come crumbling down. Amazingly, despite this tremendous onslaught, the walls remained standing for the better part of a month. It wasn't until May 18th that the Mamluks managed to break through the inner walls of Acre and commence their attack on those still inside.

Knowing that a terrible fate lay in store for them if they were captured, most of the civilian population of the city rushed off to ships that were waiting in the ports to make a desperate escape to Europe. The Teutonic Knights, Knights Templar, Knights Hospitaller, in the meantime, fought on, all the while helping to facilitate this exodus. The outnumbered knights—the only thing that stood between the Mamluks and the fleeing civilian population—were relentlessly butchered until the last living contingent was forced to hole up in the headquarters of the Knights Templar—the Templar House.

The Templar House was near the main port of Acre, and those civilians who had literally missed the boat and failed to be evacuated also sought refuge in this last bastion of Crusader might. Even though their cause most certainly seemed lost, the Crusaders were able to ferociously repel the invaders' repeated attempts to seize this last fortification. Sultan Khalil (the previous sultan had died at the end of 1290) was tired of losing too many men for this one last prize. He reached out to the beleaguered defenders and promised them that if they laid down their arms, they would all be granted safe passage out of Acre.

The Knights Templar, Knights Hospitaller, and Teutonic Knights considered this to be the best chance to defend the lives of those they were sworn to protect. They finally relented and took the sultan at his word. It is not known whether the sultan meant to keep his pledge or not, as his subordinates lacked restraint, making the knights immediately regret their decision. It is said that as soon as the knights laid down their arms, Mamluk troops poured in and engaged in rapacious behavior against the civilians who the knights were attempting to protect.

There is no nice way to put this except to simply say it. The Mamluks began preying upon women and, in some instances, even small children. Disgusted and infuriated, the knights took hold of their weapons and began slaughtering the intruders. The fury of the knights was so effective that the Mamluks were completely driven from their midst. This forced the siege of the Templar House to commence once again.

Determined to get back inside, the Mamluk engineers placed bombs outside the building and blew the outer wall open. The debauched warriors then flooded in, ready for round two of their depravity. But as if some desperate Christian's prayer had just been answered, as soon as the enemy was under the roof of the Templar House, the whole building collapsed, instantly killing all inside. Templars, Hospitallers, and Teutonic Knights, as well as all of those who were under their protection, were simply no more. Acre had fallen, but there would be no debauched abuse of its last Crusader residents.

The small batch of Teutonic Knights who had managed to flee the scene ended up in Venice before being redeployed to join the rest of their brethren in the Baltic. The Teutonic Knights who fled the city of Acre were fortunate enough to have a place waiting for them outside of the Middle East.

The other orders were not quite so lucky, and the Knights Templar, in particular, found life outside of the Levant very difficult. The Knights Templar had returned to France only to be despised for their perceived failures in the Middle East. As well as being despised for their military defeat, they were also under deep suspicion by the French Crown as to how they had amassed such a fortune.

The Knights Templar, you see, had indeed accrued a large amount of money. During their time overseas, they had essentially worked as a bank, doling out loans to various lords and nobles for several decades.

If you were a member of the nobility seeking to lead a crusade, there was no one better than the Knights Templar to help finance the expense. Even King Philip IV of France himself owed a considerable sum to the Knights Templar.

But rather than make good on his debt, he decided to have the knights arrested instead. The French king resented the Templars' wealth, and he also did not think it was such a good idea to have a restive band of hardcore fighters in his kingdom. And so, just like the Teutonic Knights were expelled from Hungary, King Philip was ready to take on the Knights Templar.

And so, one fine day—Friday the 13th, no less—in October of 1307, the French king's troops burst into the Templars' residence and placed all of the knights inside under their custody. The Knights Templar were then tortured until they made confessions of blasphemy.

The tortured Templars were forced to claim, among other things, that they had denied Christ and had participated in rituals of "spitting" on crucifixes. Most, however, consider these to be false confessions that were made under duress. In fact, the grand master of the order later recanted as he was being burned at the stake.

Did the French king or the pope feel any real remorse for the fate of the Knights Templar after it was all said and done? It is hard to say. Nevertheless, the Knights Templar had been destroyed. This act made the leadership of the Teutonic Knights realize that their toehold in the Baltic was not just an important frontier of Christendom but also vital to the very survival of the knighthood itself.

Chapter 3 – Taking on Lithuania

"It was not reason that besieged Troy. It was not reason that sent forth the Saracen from the desert to conquer the world; that inspired the Crusades; that instituted the monastic orders. It was not reason that produced the Jesuits. Above all, it was not reason that created the French Revolution. Man is only great when he acts from the passions; never irresistible but when he appeals to the imagination."

-Benjamin Disraeli

In the aftermath of the destruction of their fellow monastic order—the Knights Templar—the Teutonic Knights strove to consolidate their gains in Eastern Europe. They came to a crossroads in 1308 when tensions over the fate of Danzig and Pomerelia brought down the wrath of Poland.

This tension began the previous year when the Teutonic Knights took control of Danzig. They initially did so to aid the Poles, who were being opposed by the Margraviate of Brandenburg—a principality of the Holy Roman Empire—which was trying to stake its claim in the region. This principality of the Holy Roman Empire was actively supporting a homegrown rebellion of Pomerelians. It was into this complicated drama that the knights would enter. The Teutonic

Knights stormed into Danzig on November 13th, 1308, and a bloodbath ensued, which left many civilians dead.

If this was not bad enough, shortly thereafter, the knights began to argue with the Polish king over the administration of the captured city. As these tensions threatened to boil over, the pope made the situation even more volatile in the fall of 1309 when he issued a papal bull that authorized an investigation into the Teutonic Knights' activities. Among other things, the knights were charged with "insulting our Redeemer, shaming all the faithful and damaging the faith," not to mention the charge that the knights had "killed more than ten thousand people with the sword, inflicting death on whining infants in cradles whom even the enemy of faith would have spared."

The actual death toll and whether or not the Teutonic Knights were depraved enough to strike infants in the cradle have long been disputed. Nevertheless, the Teutonic Knights had a history of mistreating the civilian populations of enemy combatants, and after the bloodbath of Danzig, the papacy was ready to bring down the hammer on the Teutonic Order. The secular powers of Poland, as well as the papacy, were now aligning themselves to move against the Teutonic Knights.

And in the aftermath of the Templars' extermination, it no doubt seemed that the Teutonic Knights would be next. But they certainly weren't going to go down without a fight. Unlike the Knights Templar, they had their own swath of territory in the Baltic, impregnable fortresses, and a decent fighting force. Anyone who dared to try and shut the knights down by force was going to be in for a tremendous fight.

This fight took place on two fronts. A legal battle ensued alongside the martial one, as the Teutonic Knights pushed back against the charges leveled by the Vatican. All of this was happening while the Teutonic Knights pursued a continued military effort against the pagan territories surrounding their holdings so as to show the world that the knights still had a purpose (unlike the deposed Knights Templar) in defense (or furtherance) of the Christian faith.

The Teutonic Knights now put all of their focus on battling their enemies on the Lithuanian/Russian frontier. They had to do this while being wary of potential Polish aggression while their backs were turned. The Lithuanians, in the meantime, came to realize that they were essentially making a last stand as it pertained to the survival of their pagan customs and way of life. They knew that the Teutonic Knights were hellbent on forcing them to convert to Christianity no matter the cost, and the Lithuanians were just as determined to resist.

So, in this spirit of resistance, in 1316, the grand duke of Lithuania, a pagan ruler named Gediminas, cobbled together a huge force of various Lithuanian factions. Gediminas had become the grand duke after his brother Vytenis abruptly perished the previous year. Gediminas quickly proved himself to be an excellent strategist, and he was able to align this last pagan outpost with other non-Christian powers. He established relations with the Tatars of Eastern Europe, who, in turn, established a link with the Mongolian warlord successors of Genghis Khan.

Genghis Khan himself, of course, had passed away nearly one hundred years before in 1227. His successors continued to spill out of Central Asia and into Eastern Europe. By bolstering his relations with Tartars and Mongolians, Gediminas took a pigeonholed Lithuania and transformed it into not only a more powerful adversary for the Teutonic Knights but also a greater threat to European Christendom in general. But the diplomacy of Gediminas did not end there since he also reached out to none other than the Byzantine Empire. He even managed to get an Orthodox-styled metropolitan installed in Lithuania. Yes, Gediminas seemed to be trying to box the Teutonic Knights in with a series of wide-ranging strategic alliances.

It was with these concerns in mind that the Teutonic Knights began a major offensive against the Lithuanians in the summer of 1320. Their efforts were initially successful, and the Teutonic Knights were able to march into the deep reaches of Lithuania. Gediminas's forces took a considerable hit, and many pagan prisoners of war were captured.

But as the knights attempted to exit the Lithuanian frontier with their captives in tow, they were ambushed by pagan fighters. A terrific battle ensued in which twenty-nine Teutonic Knights were killed. This would have been considered a relatively manageable loss when the Teutonic Knights were at the height of their power, but their numbers and resources were in decline. Having said that, twenty-nine lost knights put a significant dent into their immediate efforts. So, in consideration of all of this, the Teutonic Knights made efforts to recruit additional troops from the surrounding regions.

They forged a backup militia drafted from regions such as Bohemia, the Rhineland, and Silesia. The knights' recruitment was tremendously successful, and they managed to cobble together a large infantry to aid them in their efforts. With this reconstituted force, the Teutonic Knights returned to Lithuania in 1322. Here, the Teutonic Knights fell back on their old heavy-handed tactics, destroying not only Lithuanian military encampments but also whole settlements, leading to a large number of civilian casualties.

The Teutonic Knights were clearly trying to force the Lithuanians to surrender. But the scorched-earth tactics only emboldened the Lithuanian resistance even more. And the Lithuanian Grand Duke Gediminas had a surprise in store for the Teutonic Knights. He managed to send a huge army to the knights' own home base in Livonia. The pagans destroyed much of the Livonian countryside and took thousands of prisoners of war back to their territory.

Interestingly enough, even while all of this was going on, Gediminas was reaching out to the pope, claiming that he was willing to convert himself and his whole realm to Christianity if the pope would convince the Teutonic Knights to back off. In reality, the grand duke had no intention of converting; just as many other pagan rulers had done in the past, he was attempting to play both sides.

Gediminas thought that if he kept the pope interested in the hope that soon there would be a wholesale, bloodless conversion of the Lithuanians, the pontiff would urge the Teutonic Knights to restrain themselves. This would then give the Lithuanian militants more time to prepare themselves for an even greater, long-term struggle.

The winter of 1323 was extremely cold, so cold that the Teutonic Knights canceled any offensives they had planned for the new year. The next several years would be a veritable stalemate in which various skirmishes would erupt without a decisive outcome. The Teutonic Knights would not embark on a major offensive inside Lithuania until the spring of 1336. At that time, the Teutonic Knights, backed up by thousands of German, Austrian, and French troops, stormed into Lithuania.

Their goal was to take out a Lithuanian military fortification known as the Pilenai hill fort. This fort was full of Lithuanian militants, as well as plenty of Lithuanian civilians. The siege commenced against the fortress on February 25th, 1336. The civilians were actually seeking safety from the brutality of the Teutonic Knights within this armed citadel. Yes, in what could be viewed as a parallel between the last stand of the Teutonic Knights in the Templar House in Acre in 1291, here you had non-Christian pagans holed up in a fortress with Lithuanian fighters doing their best to protect those under their charge.

The Teutonic Knights laid siege to the fort, and soon the walls began to give way. It was then that the desperate Lithuanian defenders made the decision to commit mass suicide. Rather than surrender or allow themselves to be killed by the enemy, they put their own families to the sword before they, too, took their own life.

Just to put this into perspective, consider how the 20th century was shocked by the mass suicide at Jonestown, in which 918 people perished. That was certainly bad enough. But some estimates say that the mass suicide of these pagan Lithuanians was several times that number.

If the Teutonic Knights and their allies expected to bring back prisoners of war and their confiscated belongings, they must have been disappointed. Because by the time they made their way into the compound, nothing but rubble and countless dead bodies were there to greet them.

The pagan Lithuanians had yet to write down their own unique histories, and those who killed themselves at this siege would most certainly have been unable to regardless. But we do have a written record of this event compiled by one of the Teutonic Knights' own chroniclers, a man whose name comes down to us as Wigand of Marburg. Since this person was in the employ of the Teutonic Knights, one would most likely expect his interpretation of events to be favorable to the Teutonic Knights.

But even this pro-Teutonic retelling of events paints a pretty horrendous picture. Wigand tells us, "Upon seeing the Christian army the idolators [Lithuanian pagans] became very afraid and lost hope of defending the castle. They threw a heap of the wealth into the fire and killed themselves." Yes, as Wigand tells it, the Lithuanians knew that a terrible fate no doubt awaited them and decided to destroy themselves along with all of their possessions. They may have been bested in battle, but they were not going to allow the Teutonic Knights to have any of the traditional spoils of war.

This was indeed a decisive defeat for the Lithuanians, but they were not quite down for the count. Fighting between the two factions would continue over the next couple of years. A brief cessation in the conflict emerged when Gediminas brokered a truce with the Livonian Knights in 1338. The grand Lithuanian strategist Gediminas passed away just a few years later, in 1341.

He had sought to buy time for his increasingly besieged pagan kingdom, and he had succeeded. And despite all of his claims of considering Christianity, he himself was given a full pagan burial. It was then up to Gediminas's son—Algirdas—to take up the struggle. Algirdas renewed hostilities by taking over the Russian city of Pskov, thereby placing Lithuanian troops dangerously close to Livonian borders.

This led the grand master of the Teutonic Knights to seek authority to enlarge the war. The Teutonic Knights were granted permission to do this by Holy Roman Emperor Louis IV, who gave the knights the green light to conquer not only Lithuanian but also Russian lands as well—all in the name of Catholicism.

The Russians, of course, were already Christians of the Orthodox faith, but due to the schism of 1054, they were viewed as heretics by the Catholic Church. Now the Russian Orthodox Christians were once again in the crosshairs of the Teutonic Knights. The knights were determined to storm into the east, so they actually built three military highways that stretched into the Lithuanian frontier for the sole purpose of being able to speedily move in and out of Lithuania. They also launched a major recruiting drive, adding several more men to their number. These knights were then backed up by an additional force provided by the son of a Bohemian king—Charles of Moravia.

Just a year after his Gediminas's death, the new Lithuanian leader, Algirdas, went on the offensive and launched an invasion of Livonia itself. The aggressors had hoped to overwhelm their enemies, but this attack was ultimately repulsed by a united force of both Estonians and Livonians.

The next major offensive conducted by Algirdas and his Lithuanian army occurred in 1345. They drove deep into Livonia, killing many and taking many more captive before they returned to Lithuanian territory. This was followed by another raid in 1346 and then another in 1347. At this point, it is said that the Lithuanians were in possession of literally thousands of hostages. The Lithuanians seemed to have the upper hand, but in 1348, all operations ground to a halt due to the sudden outbreak of a plague known as the Black Death.

It is said that the Black Death first arrived in Europe when twelve merchant ships just back from Asia arrived at the port of Messina, Sicily. Those who greeted the travelers at the dock were shocked to find that the ships were full of dead passengers, and those who survived were terribly ill, with gangrene-like infections dripping with blood and pus. Horrified, the city authorities ordered what they referred to as "death ships" to depart lest the illness spread.

Such actions might be considered a little cutthroat on the Sicilians' part since they did not seem to care too much about the fate of the ships' ailing passengers. But even so, their attempt to avoid catching the disease that was carried on board these "death ships" was futile because it had already spread from the ships to the people on the docks. Soon, the whole city was infected.

As a testament to how contagious the dreaded illness was, by the following year, the Black Death had become widespread. In the end, this disease would kill between twenty-five million and fifty million people in Europe. Despite this, the Teutonic Knights were able to rally and soon were conducting what they viewed to be "preventative strikes" into the Lithuanian heartland. These strikes were overseen by none other than the grand master of the Teutonic Order—Winrich von Kniprode.

Grand Master Winrich von Kniprode proved to be quite formidable and would serve as the leader of the order for a little over three decades, from 1351 to 1382. He knew that since the plague had already weakened his enemies and whittled down their numbers that he was best served playing the long game and waging a war that was essentially one of attrition. He knew that if he played his cards right and was able to outmaneuver his enemy and slowly wait it out that they would eventually collapse of their own accord.

The grand master also strengthened his own ties diplomatically while he was at it. In 1366, he managed to secure a lasting peace with Poland in the so-called "Peace of Danzig." With the threat of an attack from the Poles eliminated, the Teutonic Knights could better focus on the Lithuanians. These efforts then came to a climax in the spring of 1370 during the ferocious Battle of Rudau.

Near the settlement of Rudau, just north of the Prussian city of Konigsberg, the Teutonic Knights engaged in a major confrontation with the Lithuanian militants. The Lithuanian forces consisted of a combination of Lithuanians and Samogitians, as well as Ruthenians and even some Tartars. This group managed to storm Rudau Castle and set the fortress on fire.

Grand Master Winrich von Kniprode responded by sending the main bulk of his forces north out of Konigsberg and engaging the Lithuanians right there in Rudau. Not a whole lot more is known about how the battle played out. We know that the fighting would have been tremendous, yet the victorious Teutonic Knights were later strangely silent about the whole affair.

The only details of this battle come down to us from a Polish priest by the name of Jan Dlugosz, but his account is not entirely trusted by historians and often not even mentioned in mainstream historical accounts. All we really know for sure is that the Lithuanians were soundly defeated, with thousands of their number killed. It is also known that Algirdas and what was left of his army were forced to flee to the vast wooded terrain of Lithuania.

There was one recorded tragedy that beset the Teutonic Knights in the aftermath of the fighting. Teutonic Marshal Henning Schindekopf attempted to pursue the enemy. One of the men from the Lithuanian rearguard hurled a spear hurled at him. The spear hit its mark, and the mortally wounded Marshal Schindekopf perished as he was rushed back to Konigsberg.

Another turning point in the conflict came in 1377 when the Lithuanian leader Algirdas passed away. Winrich von Kniprode would himself pass away just a few years later, in 1382. The Lithuanians seemed to have gotten the memo, for soon after Winrich von Kniprode's demise, they renewed their assault. The Lithuanians got within twenty-five miles of the Teutonic base at Konigsberg, but their advance stalled, and they were once again pushed back.

One advantage that the Lithuanians continued to have throughout the conflict was the location of their base of operations: they were upriver from the Teutonic Knights. This meant that it was much easier for them to lay siege to the Teutonic Knights' fortresses. Back then, cannons were in their infancy, so they were not very mobile. You see, the easiest way to move these heavy pieces of equipment was to float them downriver. Since the Teutonic Knights were downriver, it was always easier for the Lithuanians to transport cannons and other heavy siege instruments than it was for the knights. This was all well and good for the Lithuanian insurgents, but then something happened.

Algirdas's successor, Grand Duke Jogaila, grew weary of the war and decided to finally take the Christians up on their offer and convert. In 1386, he was baptized a Christian and changed his name to Wladyslaw. These actions brought all of Lithuania into the arms of Christendom. Shortly thereafter, Wladyslaw wed the queen of Poland, Jadwiga, and he would then become known as Wladyslaw II Jagiello. This marriage would lead to the Polish-Lithuanian Union.

The fact that Lithuania was now a Christian nation ended the main mission of the Teutonic Knights in the Baltic. Upon marrying the queen of Poland, Jogaila (now Wladyslaw II Jagiello) became the king of Poland. With Jagiello preoccupied with Poland, it then fell upon his cousin, Vytautas, to oversee military operations in Lithuania. Vytautas was ultimately made the grand duke of Lithuania in 1401.

After this stage was set, the old Prussians within the domain of the Teutonic Knights once again rose up in rebellion against the knights. The Teutonic Knights suspected that the Lithuanians were behind the disturbance and prepared to strike out against Lithuania. But this was not the same Lithuania that the Teutonic Knights had faced in the past. This was now a Christian nation, one that was united with Poland. The next thing the knights knew, the Poles were readying to go to war against them if they dared to engage in hostilities with Lithuania. These latest rumblings would lead to an all-out war between the Teutonic Knights and the Polish-Lithuanian Union in 1409.

Chapter 4 – Struggling to Hang On

"The question I'm always asking myself is: are we masters or victims? Do we make history, or does history make us? Do we shape the world, or are we just shaped by it? The question of do we have agency in our lives or whether we are just passive victims of events is—I think—a great question. And one that I have always tried to ask."

-Salman Rushdie

In light of Polish support for the uprising in Lithuania, the Teutonic Knights declared war on the Polish-Lithuanian Union on August 6th, 1409. This terrible confrontation was led by Teutonic Grand Master Ulrich von Jungingen, who led the Teutonic Knights from 1407 to 1410. Since the Teutonic Knights were dealing with both Poland and Lithuania, they developed a strategy in which they hoped to pick off Poland first before focusing the full scope of their might on Lithuania.

With this in mind, the knights sent a force into the Kuyavia region of Poland. Once there, the Teutonic Knights laid siege to and ultimately demolished the Polish castle at Dobrin. They then went on to defeat Polish positions at Bobrowniki and Bydgoszcz, as well as destroyed many smaller settlements along the way. The Poles were rocked by these losses, and they ultimately signed a limited truce with the knights on October 8th, 1409, which would last until at least June 24th, 1410.

This truce was mediated by King Wenceslaus IV of Bohemia. The treaty empowered King Wenceslaus to be the arbiter of what was meant to be fair terms for both sides. These terms were reached just prior to the Catholic commemoration of Lent, with both sides (one headed by Wladyslaw II Jagiello and the other by Grand Master Ulrich von Jungingen) vying to persuade King Wenceslaus that they were in the right.

For Teutonic Grand Master Jungingen's presentation of grievances to King Wenceslaus, he came with a well-documented history of turmoil in the region, which portrayed the Lithuanians as being treacherous and in violation of numerous previous treaties to both the Teutonic Knights and Poland. The report also contained a bit of unverifiable slander, in which Jungingen tried to claim that most Lithuanian Christian converts were either pagans or participators in the Orthodox faith.

The Catholic Church, of course, had been at odds with their Christian Orthodox brethren of the East for quite some time. Ever since the Eastern church and the Western church came into disagreement over everything, from the use of leavened or unleavened bread to the pope's claim of "universal jurisdiction," the Catholic Church had found the Orthodox faith to be in error.

Therefore, the Teutonic Knights' attempt to paint the Lithuanians as Orthodox was an effort to get the Catholic Church to consider them to be in error as well. It was tantamount to a smear campaign on the part of the Teutonic Knights, but at this point, they had found themselves attempting to seek whatever political high ground that they could.

On February 8th, 1410, after hearing both sides, King Wenceslaus introduced his proposed terms for a lasting peace. Wenceslaus suggested that the two sides essentially go back to the status quo from before the hostilities had occurred. Since this was viewed as being favorable to the Teutonic Knights and altogether unfavorable to Poland, the Poles were not going to agree to these stipulations.

The Polish delegation, in fact, was so irate that they managed to overstay their welcome debating Wenceslaus's decision. The annoyed potentate actually intimated that if the Poles did not back off, he would engage them in combat himself. At any rate, it was clear that any lasting peace between the two warring parties was not going to happen any time soon.

During this temporary lull in fighting, both the Teutonic Knights and the Poles prepared themselves for the next inevitable conflict. And by the end of the year, the Lithuanian-born potentate who sat on Poland's throne— Wladyslaw II Jagiello (formerly Jogaila)—came up with a grand scheme with his second-in-command, Lithuanian Grand Duke Vytautas, of how they could unify the Polish and Lithuanian armies to march on the Teutonic capital of Marienburg (which is now called Malbork and is a town within modern-day Poland).

The Teutonic Knights were under the impression that they would face intermittent fighting from either the Lithuanian or Polish but not against a united Polish-Lithuanian army coming from the same direction. As such, Grand Master Ulrich von Jungingen had his knights position themselves in a centralized location around the Polish town of Schwetz (Swiecie). The Polish-Lithuanian forces also helped to keep up the ruse that attacks would be coming from both directions by staging a series of small-scale raids on either side of the Teutonic borders.

In the meantime, however, the main contingent of combined Polish-Lithuanian soldiers was being amassed around the Polish settlement of Czerwiensk, which at that time was located about fifty miles from the Prussian border. The exact size of this army is unknown, with chroniclers leaving the exact figure up to the imagination. But if one were to wager a guess, it was most likely rather formidable and massive in scope. The force was organized and put in place around June 24th, 1410, the moment that the temporary truce between Poland and the Teutonic Knights had come to an end. By July, this force was on its way to Marienburg.

One of the anonymous chroniclers of the history of the Teutonic Order gave a fairly detailed description of what this massive fighting force was like. (Apparently, this chronicler had worked under Johann von Posilge, a well-known chronicler of the knights.)

The chronicler remarked, "[King Jagiello] gathered the Tatars, Russians, Lithuanians, and Samogitians against Christendom. So the king met with the non-Christians and with Vytautas, who came through Mazovia to aid him, and with the duchess. There was so large an army that it is impossible to describe, and it crossed from Plock toward the land of Prussia. At Thorn were the important counts of Gora and Stiborzie, whom the king of Hungary had sent especially to Prussia to negotiate the issues and controversies between the Teutonic Order and Poland; but they could do nothing about the matter and finally departed from the king, who followed his evil and divisive will to injure Christendom. He was not satisfied with the evil men of the pagans and Poles, but he had hired many mercenaries from Bohemia, Moravia, and all kinds of knights and men at arms, who against all honor and goodness and honesty went with heathendom against Christians to ravage the lands of Prussia."

Although the anonymous chronicler tells us that the enemy's army "is impossible to describe," his words give us a very good idea of just what the Teutonic Knights faced. But it was not just the knights themselves who were being threatened by this ferocious horde of fighters. Several settlements under the dominion of the Teutonic Knights were leveled as the massive armed group progressed, and many atrocities were carried out against villagers. The most egregious perpetrators seem to have been the Tartar mercenaries that tagged along with the Lithuanians. It is said that the Tatars slaughtered, tortured, raped, and otherwise preyed upon German and Polish villagers alike. These terrible acts caused many of the Polish commanders to voice their concern to King Wladyslaw II Jagiello, who ended up issuing a strong condemnation to the Tartars and demanded that they cease and desist. The Polish king attempted to make it clear that they were there to take on the Teutonic Knights, not to abuse their subjects.

But it is unclear if his words had much effect in changing the mercenaries' behavior. As the massive army approached, the Teutonic Knights finally understood what was happening, and they began to hastily reorganize their forces. They ended up leaving just a few thousand of their number at Schwetz under the command of a Teutonic Knight by the name of Heinrich von Plauen. They sent the main bulk of their army toward the enemy. The forces then collided at Tannenberg on July 15th, 1410.

Although the exact numbers are unknown, it has been said that there were tens of thousands of combatants on each side. At the outset, the Teutonic Knights tried to establish a defensive perimeter, digging trenches around their position. The trenches were camouflaged and put in place with the intent of causing their opponents' charging cavalry to fall into them. This would more than likely break a horse's legs and most likely kill its rider.

But after several hours had passed with the Polish-Lithuanian forces failing to advance, the grand master of the Teutonic Order made the fateful decision to pull back. This was done for a variety of reasons, one of which was supposedly that the sun was beginning to rise on the horizon right in front of the knights, threatening to completely obscure their vision.

This sounds reasonable enough. But pulling back right when the enemy was about to engage them would prove to be a terrible and costly mistake. For one thing, it made the knights look cowardly, almost as if they had lost their nerve and were backing off altogether. Far worse than this, however, as the Polish-Lithuanian troops advanced, they were able to take over the freshly dug trenches and use them for their own purposes.

With the enemy in control of this defensive line, the Teutonic Knights now had to cross this booby-trapped chasm themselves. This presented a terrible hazard to their own cavalry, and many of those fighting on the side of the knights would needlessly perish as a result. All things considered, this was perhaps one of the worst tactical errors in military history.

Nevertheless, the knights soldiered on. Despite the hardship involved, the knights valiantly tried to turn the tide. But there was more failure in store for them. At one point during the melee, the Lithuanians managed to psych the knights out by feigning to withdraw. The knights were excited at the idea of the Lithuanians being beaten, so they chased a group of Lithuanian cavalry as they sped off into the forest. However, as soon as the knights followed, they found a large group of Poles lying in wait, who then surged forward to greet them. The group of Teutonic Knights who dared to charge into the woods was about to be annihilated. In order to save them, the Teutonic grand master had a contingent of his knights arrange themselves in a closely grouped battle formation and march on the Polish fighters in the woods.

But even so, the Lithuanian forces were ready, and even more of their number rushed in from all sides, ferociously hacking and slicing their way through the beleaguered knights. The knights attempted to make a tactical withdraw, but they were too ensnared to get away. Making matters even worse, Grand Master Jungingen ended up perishing in the melee. It's unclear exactly how he died, although there is a fanciful legend that he was struck with Jagiello's own lance when the two leaders charged at each other.

At any rate, as soon as the Teutonic Knights realized their leader had perished on the field, the rest of them began fleeing the scene in desperate disarray. They had lost the battle, and those who remained were simply trying to cut their way through so that they could escape. Even those who successfully fled and made their way back to the

Teutonic stronghold of Marienburg soon found themselves surrounded by the enemy in their own castle.

According to writer and historian William Urban, the lowest estimate of casualties suffered by the Teutonic contingent during this one battle is an astonishing eight thousand men. As the Teutonic Knights' chronicler put it, "The army, both cavalry and infantry, was routed completely, losing goods, and honor, and the number slain was beyond numbering. May God have pity on them."

With such a crushing defeat, the Polish-Lithuanian forces were absolutely confident that they were going to wipe the knights out entirely and claim the Teutonic lands for their own. But the Teutonic Knights were not completely defeated yet. Heinrich von Plauen, the Teutonic Knight commander who had been left in charge of the smaller force of knights left at Schwetz, began to feverishly work toward salvaging what no doubt seemed to be a lost cause.

As soon as Heinrich figured out what had happened, he sent the three thousand troops that were at his command north to save Marienburg. Upon his arrival, he went from garrison to garrison and prepared them to defend the fortress at all cost. He also sent a message to the knights in Livonia to request their assistance. This last-minute maneuvering conducted by Heinrich von Plauen would truly save the day at Marienburg.

Rather than finding a wounded and beaten foe hiding out at Marienburg Castle (Malbork Castle), the Polish forces found a well-disciplined fighting force, complete with formidable cannons aimed in their direction from the battlements. It seems the Teutonic Knights were ready to blast the Polish-Lithuanian army into oblivion. Heinrich von Plauen also made sure to bring all the cattle and stores of food that he could muster into the storehouses of Marienburg Castle, with the full intention of surviving a prolonged siege.

The Poles and Lithuanians were ill-prepared for these efforts, and they found themselves low on supplies and lacking the proper siege equipment to best these embattled knights. While the Polish-

Lithuanian army dithered, Heinrich raised the stakes even further by firing off what amounted to an all-points bulletin to the princes of Germany.

The announcement read, in part:

"To all princes, barons, knights and men-at-arms and all other loyal Christians, whomever this letter reaches. We brother Heinrich of Plauen, commander of Schwetz, acting in the place of the Grand Master of the Teutonic Order in Prussia, notify you that the King of Poland and Duke Vytautas with a great force and with Saracen [Tartar] infidels have besieged Marienburg. In this siege truly all the order's forces and power are being engaged. Therefore, we ask you illustrious and noble lords to allow your subjects who wish to assist and defend us for the love of Christ and all of Christendom either for salvation or money, to come to our aid as quickly as possible so that we can drive them away."

Here, Heinrich proved himself to be a savvy medieval marketer. He essentially called his own unofficial crusade and suggested that those who fought and died for their cause, which he presented as a cause for "all of Christendom," could be rewarded with "salvation or money." During previous crusades called by previous popes, the promise of the absolution of sin for those who fought for the cause of Christianity was often presented. Here, we find Heinrich making that very suggestion himself. This announcement resulted in German troops from all over the Holy Roman Empire pouring into the region to shore up the defenses of Marienburg against the Polish-Lithuanian assault.

Nevertheless, the Polish king, Wladyslaw II Jagiello, urged his forces on. At the gates of Marienburg, he had them use the limited tools at their disposal to batter the walls of the castle. He also unleashed bands of Lithuanians on the surrounding villages to terrorize the citizens into swearing their allegiance to the Polish king. This was done in order to put pressure on the knights.

The Livonian Knights arrived on the scene shortly thereafter, however, and managed to eliminate the Lithuanian aggressors. The fact that the Livonian Knights succeeded so easily where the Teutonic Knights had failed seems to be largely due to a better battlefield strategy, as well as the fact that the Lithuanian troops were exhausted and low on supplies. The Lithuanians were simply not ready for the onslaught that these fresh-faced knights dished out to them.

After the Lithuanian militants were put down, a large force of Hungarian and German mercenaries also answered the call and unleashed their fury upon the Polish troops, decimating their ranks and even taking a top commander prisoner. What had seemed to be a glorious victory for the Polish-Lithuanian Union was quickly turning into one of its worst defeats. With Marienburg well stocked and well defended, and with the Livonian Knights, along with auxiliary forces of mercenaries, securing the surrounding countryside, Jagiello had no choice but to pull what remained of his forces back.

Now seemingly on the defensive, Jagiello had an improvised fortress constructed, which he filled with as many supplies as he could muster and surrounded it with a well-armed garrison. He was apparently ready for a standoff to commence.

Heinrich von Plauen, in the meantime, gave instructions for those under his charge to recover as much of the lost surrounding territory as they could. The Livonian Knights were able to secure many of the surrounding settlements, and by the time October rolled around, all major settlements except for the town of Thorn had been secured. This town was still under Polish-Lithuanian control, and it would become the backdrop of the peace brokered between the two warring parties.

It was an incredible feat for the knights to recover so much lost ground so quickly, yet the burning question on the minds of most of their brethren was why were the Teutonic Knights annihilated at Tannenberg? As the Teutonic chronicler seems to suggest, the most common explanation was that the Teutonic Knights at Tannenberg were simply outnumbered.

Yet this fact alone does not seem sufficient to make sense of the wholescale slaughter that the knights sustained. The Teutonic Knights, after all, were used to being outnumbered. And typically, their cautious battlefield strategy helped them to prevail even in the face of great odds. It was for this reason alone that many of the brethren began to consider other reasons for the loss.

For some, there seemed to be a hint of treason, and an idea was entertained that perhaps some of the mercenaries had switched sides at the last moment. A large portion of the Teutonic Knights' infantry during the battle were soldiers of fortune, after all, and it was not that uncommon for such fickle and easily bought fighters to have a last-minute change of heart.

For most, however, the sinking realization of the failure at Tannenberg was simply a grave miscalculation in judgment. And as much as the Teutonic Knights argued amongst themselves as to what had happened, modern historians still debate the exact cause of this colossal failure. But whatever the case may have been, it was now up to Heinrich von Plauen and the rest of the survivors to pick up the pieces.

Chapter 5 – The Peace of Thorn and its Aftermath

"The effects which follow too constant and intense a concentration upon evil are always disastrous. Those who crusade, not for God in themselves, but against the devil in others, never succeed in making the world better, but leave it either as it was, or sometimes even perceptibly worse than it was before the crusade began. By thinking primarily of evil, we tend—however excellent our intentions—to create occasions for evil to manifest itself."

-Aldous Huxley

The Peace of Thorn of 1411 would allow the knights to keep most of their landholdings, even though their once fearsome reputation had a significant dent put into it. The man who rose up from the rubble as the leading light of the knights—Heinrich von Plauen—tried his best to portray the disastrous defeat at Tannenberg as a mere setback rather than an unmitigated disaster.

Before the knights signed off on the Peace of Thorn, von Plauen attempted to raise even more troops and resources in an effort to take the fight to the Polish-Lithuanian army. Others advised him against the effort and sought to convince him to cut his losses and agree to a truce. It was believed that although the enemy was not defeated, the

Teutonic Knights had prevented the Teutonic stronghold from being overrun and the order itself from being destroyed. For those who had rallied to the knights' cause, this alone was sufficient, and most did not see the need to pursue the enemy forces. On the contrary, such a thing seemed foolhardy at best since if their efforts failed, the Teutonic Order most likely would be extinguished.

Heinrich von Plauen, in the meantime, was not a grand master of the Teutonic Order. He had taken the authority of one on an emergency basis, but a grand master had to be officially elected to lead the knights. This election occurred in November of 1410, and with little surprise, Heinrich von Plauen was elected. He had proved himself as a more than able commander and was viewed in heroic terms by his subordinates, so this came as little surprise. Now, the question on everyone's mind was if Heinrich von Plauen would take the war to the enemy by marching on Poland to dethrone King Jagiello as he had intended. Or would he cut his losses, agree to an immediate truce, and focus on rebuilding the Teutonic Knights and their domain?

Initially, the new grand master seemed ready for all-out war. In the first few weeks after his inauguration, he sent an expeditionary force to Thorn, which was able to retake some minor fortresses. But there were setbacks as well, such as the new marshal of the order—Michael Küchmeister—being captured. On top of that, one of his contingents of knights was overrun by Polish forces.

Once Michael Küchmeister returned to his fellow brothers of the order after being ransomed, he became one of the most vocal voices in Grand Master Heinrich von Plauen's ear, insisting that widening the war against the Polish-Lithuanian Union was a mistake. In the meantime, Jagiello's righthand man in Lithuania, his cousin Vytautas, arrived with Lithuanian reinforcements.

Due to all of these factors, the grand master of the Teutonic Knights finally gave in to his colleagues, and efforts to negotiate a truce began in earnest. These talks led to the signing of the First Peace of

Thorn on February 1st, 1411. The signing of this agreement ended hostilities and sent the armed encampments back to their respective territories, but there were ramifications.

Peace was secure, but home economies were almost ruined. And on top of this, according to the terms of the agreement, the Teutonic Knights were forced to pay indemnities to the Polish-Lithuanian Union. This caused the Teutonic Knights to raise taxes on their subject peoples just to keep the government they shepherded up and running. It is said that the citizens naturally resented this action, and great tension between the knights and their subjects resulted.

According to one rather sensational-sounding story, the knights actually targeted a prominent citizen who refused to pay the higher taxes. A man named Konrad Lezkau is said to have openly criticized the knights' actions. This was a bold move since the knights were not above punishing rebellious subjects with everything from throwing them into a dungeon to giving them a good old public flogging. Yes, the Middle Ages were indeed brutal times. There is a reason someone shouting, "Hey buddy! I'm about to go medieval on you!" is considered a threat!

Nevertheless, the knights apparently seemed willing to listen to Konrad's concerns and even invited Konrad and a few similarly minded citizens to have dinner with them so that they could discuss the new measures in person. Relieved that the knights were being so reasonable, Konrad and his fellow noblemen agreed to join the Teutonic Knights at their castle for dinner.

According to this tale, on the day of the dinner date, the guests were met at the door by the knights' court jester, who uttered a rather puzzling remark. The jester looked the group over and darkly suggested that "if only they knew" what the Teutonic Knights "were cooking," they just might reconsider dining with them.

At least one of the shrewder members is said to have taken this as a veiled threat and found a reason to turn back and go home. The rest, however, just shrugged off the jest and went ahead with their meeting as planned. Upon taking their place at the table, rather than being served good food with a side of pleasant conversation, they were openly berated by the knights. This arguing match then turned to bloodshed when the knights supposedly took their swords and made short work of their visitors.

As shocking as all of this sounds, it must once again be stressed that no one knows how much of this is just fanciful folklore and how much—if any—of it is true. But the fact that the knights were painted in such grim terms—even if the story is more myth than reality—no doubt comes from the fact that draconian measures were indeed enacted after the Peace of Thorn. And it is known that the Teutonic Knights were capable of being some pretty grim taskmasters when it came to their own subjects.

The peasant class suffered the most since many of their farms had been decimated by the Polish-Lithuanian forces during their previous rampage through the countryside, particularly since they burned everything in their wake. The harvest season of 1412 was very poor since farmers were still suffering from burned-out soil and a lack of proper supplies and equipment.

A bad harvest translated into less wealth for those immediately above the peasant farmer class, and less wealth meant less taxable revenue for the Teutonic Knights, who were desperate to pay off their war indemnities. As a result, von Plauen actually failed to make the third payment in a timely manner, prompting outrage (at least feigned outrage) on the part of Polish King Jagiello.

King Sigismund of Hungary, however, offered to mediate the dispute. After delegations met near Hungary's border in March of 1412, all was made right again. During this meeting, the final terms of the Peace of Thorn were hammered out, such as the demarcation of the Samogitian border, lingering prisoners of war, and, of course, the exact protocols of how the Teutonic Knights were to pay the war indemnities that had been foisted upon them.

Sigismund worked to smooth out the differences between the two parties, and he managed to get an agreement to send a commission to figure out the exact borders of Samogitia. He also managed to get both sides to agree to swap their prisoners of war over the next several months. Most importantly, for the Teutonic Knights' floundering economic position, Sigismund got a reduction in the overall indemnity that the knights were ordered to pay.

Yet, for the grand master of the Teutonic Order, von Plauen, all of these efforts were largely seen as a means to buy more time. And once his forces were reconstituted, and the Teutonic Order was in a position of strength, Heinrich von Plauen fully intended to strike out at his adversaries and bring back honor to the faltering Teutonic Knights by force.

But as Grand Master Heinrich von Plauen was preparing for war, his own subordinates turned against him and staged a coup. Led by Grand Marshal Michael Küchmeister, the plotting knights stormed Plauen's own bedchambers at Marienburg and essentially placed the grand master under arrest with little resistance.

Even though Grand Master Heinrich von Plauen was the avenging hero in the aftermath of Tannenberg, as he had saved the order from complete destruction, the knights were desperate to avoid a continuation of the conflict, which they felt would only lead to further disaster. Under duress, Heinrich von Plauen finally listened to reason and tendered his formal resignation in January of 1414. He was then replaced by Michael Küchmeister, who was elevated to the role of grand master shortly thereafter. These actions sealed the fate of the Teutonic Knights for the next several years, with Grand Master Küchmeister swearing to abide by the full terms of the Peace of Thorn.

Küchmeister figured that Polish King Jagiello would be receptive to these developments. But instead of showing approval, the Polish king actually called for Heinrich von Plauen to be given back the role of grand master and disparaged Michael Küchmeister as being a usurper to the title. As it turned out, two things that King Jagiello despised more than anything were cowards and traitors. In a more pragmatic sense, however, he also knew that rejecting Küchmeister could only help his long game against the Teutonic Knights.

This spread confusion in the ranks, as some knights began to reconsider Heinrich von Plauen for the role of grand master. Michael Küchmeister was not about to have that. In order to ensure that the matter was not forced, he had Heinrich von Plauen placed back into his custody. If Jagiello's aim was to sow further discord and confusion among the Teutonic Knights, he was wildly successful.

But worse was in store for Grand Master Michael Küchmeister. When the newly installed grand master met with Jagiello in April of 1414 to discuss the status of Samogitia and other territories still in dispute, Jagiello took an even harsher stance. Küchmeister had thought that the Polish king would be pleased that he had sidelined the war hawk Heinrich von Plauen, but he found that his efforts had only made him look both weak and treacherous in the eyes of the monarch, two qualities that he despised.

In order to test this perceived weakness, King Jagiello drove a harder bargain, demanding that the Teutonic Knights not only give up their claim on Samogitia but also on lands in both Pomerelia and Culm. This was too much for Grand Master Küchmeister to bear; he knew that giving up so much territory would be tantamount to the dissolution of the Teutonic Order. But since King Jagiello had just drawn a line in the sand, refusal to comply would mean war. Unable to concede, Michael Küchmeister was, ironically enough, now forced to carry out the very war for which he had deposed Grand Master Heinrich von Plauen.

Chapter 6 – The Stage is Set

"I entreat masters to live a good life and faithfully to instruct their scholars, especially that they may love God and learn to give themselves to knowledge, in order to promote his honor, the welfare of the state. And their own salvation, but not for the sake of avarice or the praise of man."

-Jan Hus

Grand Master Küchmeister had ousted Heinrich von Plauen to avoid a conflict, yet by the summer of 1414, a war between the Teutonic Knights and the Polish-Lithuanian Union was more imminent than ever. And now the knights were in an even weaker position than they would have been had Küchmeister allowed Heinrich von Plauen's plans for war proceed unhindered.

Nevertheless, Küchmeister was now the man in charge, and he had to defend the Teutonic domain accordingly. His first effort to solidify the Teutonic position was to send troops to the province of Culm in order to block the path of incoming Polish-Lithuanian troops.

In July of 1414, the Polish-Lithuanian forces arrived at Osterode, East Prussia. The knights' adversaries were ruthless on their march, indiscriminately slaughtering civilians on their way through the surrounding region. It was a dire situation, but Grand Master

Küchmeister had taken an important precaution prior to the invasion. He had seized as many foodstuffs as he could and burned the rest, making sure that the invading army would not have the resources to feed themselves once they arrived. This was why this renewed conflict was known as the "Hunger War."

Along with severe hunger, the Polish-Lithuanian troops were also struck with a severe epidemic of dysentery. Despite what looked like an easy advance on the Polish-Lithuanians' part, the huge armies were forced to make a tactical withdraw.

This latest outbreak of fighting ended in October of 1414 when direct papal mediation brought about what was essentially a ceasefire between the two belligerents. Terms were hammered out in the city of Strasbourg, which rendered a two-year truce known as the Treaty of Strasbourg. But once again, all this did for the Teutonic Knights was buy them some extra time.

This was time that Grand Master Küchmeister knew must be spent building up his forces before the next assault arrived. Since the ranks of the Teutonic Knights had significantly dwindled, the order was relying more and more upon hired mercenaries for support. These mercenaries had to be paid, and the payment for their services was creating a serious drain on the economy of the Teutonic dominion.

To the great dismay of the clergy, Grand Master Küchmeister gathered up all of the precious metals from the local churches and had them melted down just to be able to mint coins. Even with this influx of silver, he was still only able to mint coins of a debased value due to the limited precious metals available. This was barely enough to be able to keep the hired mercenaries in the employ of the Teutonic Knights. And ultimately, the debased coins put into circulation only helped to damage the prestige of the order since it served as an indication of just how far they had fallen.

However, the fortunes of the knights began to change when a new pope—Martin V—came to power in 1417. This pope saw the dire condition of the Teutonic Order. He took pity on them and immediately sought to use his influence to prevent their collapse. In December of 1417, he sent out instructions to both the Teutonic Knights and the Polish-Lithuanian Union that they were to abide by the treaty made in 1414 until further notice. This essentially extended the ceasefire that would have expired without this papal authorization.

The pope, along with King Sigismund of Hungary, then reached a final determination in January of 1420 at a conference in Silesia, in which the pope decided favorably with the Teutonic Knights. The terms of the Peace of Thorn would stand, and even Samogitia would be returned to the knights upon the passing of both the aging Jagiello and Vytautas.

The Polish delegation was enraged at the pope's decisions. They especially took umbrage at the fact that Samogitia would be taken from the heirs of Jagiello and Vytautas. Thus, the Polish found themselves preparing for war. Before all-out war erupted, Jagiello attempted to reach out to Pope Martin V one more time in a vain attempt to get the pontiff to change his mind. The pope was resolute, however, and insisted that there was nothing more he could do.

As the Polish-Lithuanian Union prepared to strike, Grand Master Michael Küchmeister was being pressured to step down. His leadership had been found to be lacking for quite some time. Küchmeister ended up handing in his resignation from the Teutonic Order on March 10th, 1422. He was replaced as grand master by Paul von Rusdorf.

Paul von Rusdorf made the fateful decision to dismiss many of the mercenary forces that the knights had been using for extra defense. And he did all of this right on the eve of the next outbreak of hostilities with the Polish-Lithuanian Union. Shortly after the mercenaries were dismissed, the Poles and Lithuanians stormed Osterode.

Outnumbered, the Teutonic Knights conducted a tactical withdrawal to Lobau (sometimes spelled Lubawa). The Polish-Lithuanian troops then marched on Marienburg before taking

Riesenburg and marching southward to the so-called "Chelmo Land" (also known as Culm). Here, the Polish-Lithuanian army took the town of Gollub.

Hostilities ended on September 27th, 1422, with the signing of the Treaty of Lake Menlo. This treaty had the knights agree to cease and desist claims on any territory in Lithuanian possession. This may have brought the Teutonic Knights peace on one front, but the challenge of Polish aggression still remained. There were also new—or perhaps we should say old—fronts opening up for the knights in the Balkans. King Sigismund of Hungary (who would become the Holy Roman emperor in 1433) requested the knights' assistance in 1429 and had a contingent of them redeployed to Transylvania, where the Teutonic Order had been briefly posted in the early 1200s.

They were placed here as a vanguard against the ever-increasing Turkish threat in the region. Transylvania was indeed volatile, and a skirmish with the Turks in 1432 almost decimated the Teutonic Knights posted there. Nevertheless, in 1437, Sigismund expressed an interest in having the entire Teutonic force redeployed from the Baltic to the Balkans. Such things, of course, would be easier said than done.

In the meantime, the knights who had remained in the Baltic had already fought another war with the Poles, with the Polish-Teutonic War breaking out in 1431. The drama began when Teutonic Grand Master Paul von Rusdorf entered into an agreement with Jagiello's brother Švitrigaila, who was leading a civil war against Jagiello at the time. Švitrigaila was the grand duke of Lithuania, having succeeded the previous grand duke, Vytautas, after he passed away in 1430.

Although Vytautas was old at the time, his death was sudden and unexpected. He had actually fallen from his horse, severely injuring himself. He perished from his wounds approximately two weeks later.

At any rate, the election of Švitrigaila as the grand duke of Lithuania immediately brought down the wrath of Poland since it had been previously promised that no successor to the Grand Duchy of

Lithuania would be claimed until it was cleared with the king of Poland.

The Teutonic Knights entered into this major rift in the Polish-Lithuanian Union, and they were more than ready to hedge their bets. They threw in their lot with Švitrigaila, and a treaty was forged between the knights and the new grand duke.

And like clockwork, in the summer of 1431, the Teutonic Knights were launching new offensives against Poland. Since a large portion of Polish troops were taking on Švitrigaila in Lithuanian territory, the knights sought to take full advantage of this by driving deep into the Polish heartland. The Teutonic offensive stalled out, however, on September 13th, 1431, when the knights were delivered a sound defeat at the Battle of Dabki.

This defeat led to the signing of yet another temporary truce between the warring parties. Further negotiations would then lead to the longer-lasting Truce of Leczyca, which was hammered out in 1433. That same fateful year, Sigismund was finally elected as Holy Roman emperor. Less than a year later, shockwaves would be sent through Europe when eighty-year-old King Jagiello of Poland literally caught his death from cold and perished in May of 1434.

The Polish king was apparently looking for some peace and respite from the nonstop turmoil of his kingdom, so he took a moment to take a nice stroll through the forest. However, it was a bit too cold for the aging monarch, and his faltering immune system found itself unable to fend off the fatal congestion that beset his lungs. The death of Jagiello opened up a fresh crisis of succession; it didn't help matters that the dispute over the succession in Lithuanian was still unresolved.

Poland's line of succession fell upon Jagiello's son Wladyslaw III. But since Jagiello's heir was not of the traditional Polish line, there was some pushback from the Polish nobles who wished to revert back to Polish royalty upon Jagiello's death. Jagiello, of course, was of Lithuanian stock and a usurper—albeit an incredibly successful one—to the traditional throne of Poland. It's not that he did anything underhanded or anything like that. He had married the queen of Poland; therefore, he was the king of Poland.

But nevertheless, there were those who still looked at him as a usurper merely because of his Lithuanian heritage. There was a nationalistic sense of tribalism afoot in Poland at the time, and no matter what Jagiello did *or* even who he married, he was simply not viewed as being "one of them." And despite the fact that Jagiello had been on the Polish throne for decades, there were those who sought to block his heirs from creating a dynasty.

Since Wladyslaw III was only ten years old at the time of his succession, this child-king was not much of a match against those who opposed him. But fortunately for him, he had a powerful backer in the form of a highly influential cardinal named Zbigniew Oleśnicki, who championed the cause of allowing Jagiello's original plans for succession to go forth.

In the aftermath of Jagiello's death, Teutonic Grand Master Paul von Rusdorf sought to get the Teutonic Knights' brother order in Livonia—the Livonian Knights—to strengthen their ties to Švitrigaila. As such, Rusdorf began deploying several Teutonic Knights, as well as other hired mercenaries, to Livonia in an attempt to help prop up Švitrigaila in nearby Lithuania. Among these redeployments was one Sigismund Korybut, who was said to have been "one of the most accomplished generals of the era."

Korybut is an interesting figure who cut his teeth fighting alongside the so-called heretics known as the Hussites. The Hussites were followers of a man named Jan Hus, who had been burned at the stake for his alleged heresy several years before. The Hussites were marked men in the eyes of the Vatican, and they were actively hunted down by Catholic forces. The movement was centered around Prague and other Czech lands that were then part of Greater Bohemia, which was, in turn, part of the Holy Roman Empire.

The Hussites were essentially Proto-Protestants, as they had emerged around one hundred years prior to the Reformation. However, unlike the later reformer Martin Luther, the Hussites did not have any meaningful backers within the Holy Roman Empire. Thus, the Catholic Church was able to put all of the power at its disposal to correct what it viewed as a rebellious and heretical sect.

Sigismund Korybut had begun to work on negotiations between the Hussites and the Catholic powers when he had a falling-out with the very Hussites he was attempting to represent. Korybut had to flee Bohemia, and he attempted to reach Lithuania. He was intercepted by the Teutonic Knights in Prussia, however, and while in Teutonic custody, the knights got him to agree to aid them in their machinations with Švitrigaila.

If you can recall, Lithuania was in the grip of a civil war, with Švitrigaila on one side and the man whom King Jagiello had chosen to be on Lithuania's throne—Zygimantas Kestutaitis—on the other. Zygimantas was also known by his baptismal name of "Sigismund," which was a common name at the time. The Teutonic Knights had hoped that by using that the other Sigismund—that is Sigismund Korybut—who was also a native Lithuanian, they would be able to draw troops away from the Zygimantas faction and bring them over to the Švitrigaila side.

Korybut, along with a coalition of Teutonic Knights and Švitrigaila's army, arrived on the scene near the Swieta River in September of 1435. In what was no doubt a do-or-die moment, he and his men prepared to launch an assault on Zygimantas's base of operations at Vilnius.

Švitrigaila was not ready for an all-out assault, so he had his troops move to higher ground in the vicinity of the settlement of Pabaiska. Here, the coalition army literally circled the wagons and created a makeshift fortress, practically daring their opponents to attack. Once Zygimantas's forces approached, subsequent skirmishes convinced the coalition that they were outgunned.

It must be kept in mind that Zygimantas's army did not just consist of native Lithuanians. On the contrary, there were also Polish troops and Tatars, who, for various reasons, supported the cause of Zygimantas. Realizing that they were heavily outnumbered, the coalition army of Teutonic Knights and Lithuanians began a tactical withdrawal. As they made their retreat, a group of Livonian Knights attempted to transfer themselves to the rearguard.

While they were repositioning themselves, Zygimantas's forces charged the brief opening in their opponents' lines. As the armies collided, the greatly outnumbered coalition was decimated. Švitrigaila and a portion of the coalition were able to escape, but thousands of Teutonic and Livonian Knights were not so lucky. And during the melee, Korybut himself was fatally wounded.

It is said that Korybut was brought directly to Zygimantas as he breathed his last breath. Truth be told, Korybut would have preferred fighting by Zygimantas's side, but he only managed to join his ranks as a corpse when his body was retrieved. This final blow to the knights and the Švitrigaila coalition ensured that Zygimantas would be the grand duke of Lithuania. And despite all of the Teutonic Knights' hopes to separate Lithuania from Poland, the Polish-Lithuanian Union would endure.

Chapter 7 – Standing at the Precipice

"Evil isn't the real threat to the world. Stupid is just as destructive as evil. Maybe more so. And it's a hell of a lot more common. What we really need is a crusade against stupid. That might actually make a difference."

-Jim Butcher

Sigismund Kestutaitis—otherwise known simply as "Zygimantas"—was first made the grand duke of Lithuania in 1432. It wasn't until 1435, however, that Zygimantas emerged as the undisputed ruler of Lithuania and was once again affirmed as being under the direct jurisdiction of Poland and its new boy-king, Wladyslaw III. With these matters settled and paganism just about extinct in Europe, the Teutonic Knights struggled to find a purpose. The crusade against Lithuania was over.

And upon its conclusion, it seemed as if the Teutonic Knights might be off the battlefield for good. The knights primarily spent the ensuing years consumed with bitter infighting in the order. This infighting was the most pernicious in Livonia, where the governance of the once-mighty Livonian Knights had become so volatile that local bishops, abbots, and nobles created the Livonian Confederation as a means of establishing some order from the outside. This confederation essentially raised up those previously subject to the Livonian Knights as equal partners in the affairs of the order.

Grand Master Paul von Rusdorf was so upset at these developments that he briefly considered launching an offensive against the Livonian Knights and taking their fortresses by force! He very quickly backed away from this idea, fully realizing that it was not only ludicrous and impractical but that it also would have scandalized the order so badly that even a victorious outcome would have been a wound from which the order as a whole would most likely never recover.

All the same, Paul von Rusdorf's greatest fear—that the trend in Livonia would spread to his own realm—was well founded. In 1440, the Teutonic Knights faced their own version of discontent when the well-to-do nobles of their dominion rose up to form the Prussian Confederation. Delegates from the Prussian Confederation confronted the grand master with demands to reform taxation, curb military levies, and root out corruption.

Grand Master Paul von Rusdorf was infuriated at what was happening, but he largely ignored the problem. He then passed the baton to the next grand master, Konrad von Erlichshausen, in 1441. Grand Master Konrad von Erlichshausen seemed like he was a Teutonic Knight who had come right out of central casting. He was in his early forties at the time of his election and was said to have been handsome with a regal bearing. He was also outgoing and extremely charismatic. Along with looking the part, he had played the part of a leader as well; he had been a field commander in countless past skirmishes.

With the election of this new grand master, the Teutonic Order desperately hoped that it would be able to turn the page on some of its past failures as an institution. Von Erlichshausen also wanted to signify to the region that strong leadership was back.

Konrad von Erlichshausen tried to instill this view by going on a grand tour of all of Prussia, visiting all of the leading lights of his realm to let them know that a strong leader had finally arrived on the scene. He also met with the Livonian grand master, and after a long discussion, the two were able to work out their differences enough to reinstate the bond that the two orders had previously shared with each other. Relations were normalized between the orders in the fall of 1442.

That same year, Konrad also introduced internal reforms to the order, which sought to better control the finances of the monastic state. It was stipulated that the knights could not accumulate wealth and valuables or keep their wealth unknown to the brotherhood. Every member of the order was to give an open account of his own personal wealth. Konrad viewed the order as a financial collective, and as such, nothing was to be secret when it came to valuables or possessions.

These measures were taken so seriously that if a knight were to pass away and it was discovered that he actually had a higher net worth than was reported, his wealth would be immediately confiscated and turned over to the order. It was also recommended that the knight be posthumously punished by not giving him a proper burial. Instead of being interred with dignity, the knight was to be given an unmarked grave.

Grand Master Konrad was also concerned with the behavior of his knights when they left the fortified monastery and mingled with the local citizens of the surrounding towns. He insisted that when the knights were abroad, they should always wear the mantle and insignia of the Teutonic Order to serve as a reminder to others and to themselves of who they were and of the vows—particularly the vow of chastity—to which they had sworn to abide. Maintaining chastity among the brethren, as it turns out, was something that Konrad was quite concerned with, and he spoke at great length about it.

In 1442, he declared, "We decree and order—wish and bid that superiors of our order—shall truly and diligently admonish the commanders to punish deliberate unchastity. And which commander or officeholder therein is found negligent after the truth is established according to the 'Book of Our Order,' that commander or officeholder shall be punished with the same penance with which his unchaste subordinate should have been punished; moreover, the unchaste brother shall not escape punishment."

Konrad was obviously a strict taskmaster, but his iron will helped keep the knighthood in shape. And Grand Master Konrad would administer the Teutonic Knights just as he saw fit until his passing in 1449. His own nephew—Ludwig von Erlichshausen—was elected as the next grand master.

While appreciating his uncle's efforts of instituting discipline, Ludwig von Erlichshausen felt that the biggest challenge to the order was an ever-increasing malaise throughout the rank-and-file knights. For him, it was not discipline that was the main problem the order faced but rather an overall lack of morale among the knighthood. Ludwig felt that the order had completely lost its sense of purpose and needed to re-exert itself in a powerful way.

The most logical means of doing so would be to somehow take part in another major crusade. Waging war against the Turks in the Balkans was a prominent topic of conversation. The Turks had slowly advanced into the Balkans and had managed to almost completely surround what was left of the Byzantine Empire. The Byzantines, of course, were the remnant of the Eastern Roman Empire, and their great capital of Constantinople (modern-day Istanbul, Turkey) was the center of the Christian Orthodox faith.

Crusades had been launched to aid the Byzantines from the very beginning; in fact, the First Crusade's main objective was to aid Byzantium, as well as recover the lost Christian territory in the Holy Land. Now, centuries later, the Byzantines truly were on their last legs, and a last-gasp effort was made to cobble together a new Crusade to rescue them once again.

However, these efforts would not amount to much, and what little aid they wrought would be too late to be of any consequence. Constantinople would ultimately be overrun by the Ottoman Turks in October of 1453, denying the Teutonic Knights and all other Crusaders the chance to defend this Christian bulwark of old. But almost as soon as word was received that Constantinople had been conquered, the Vatican and European heads of state began to speak of a new Crusade to retake what had been lost.

The Teutonic Knights pondered these things as well, but soon, they would have their hands too full at home to think of much else. By 1454, they were once again donning their suits of shining armor when the Prussian Confederation rose up to their west and sparked a lengthy conflict known as the Thirteen Years' War.

Prussian nobles had risen up in an effort to shake off the dominion of the knights, and they sought aid from the man who then sat on Poland's throne: Casimir IV Jagiellon. This Polish king granted them the favor for which they asked. So, rather than crusading to recapture Constantinople, there was suddenly plenty of fighting for the Teutonic Knights right in their own backyard.

The Polish-backed Prussian rebels were able to seize Elbing (Elblag), Danzig, and Thorn with relative ease. With the Teutonic Knights in retreat, only Stuhm, Konitz, and Marienburg remained out of the Prussian Confederation's grasp.

The Teutonic Knights were backed up by some fifteen thousand mercenaries whose services were purchased from all parts of the Holy Roman Empire. This force was led by Rudolf von Sagan, an able and experienced commander. Rudolf's army was able to break the siege that had been launched against Konitz and ended up defeating the Polish-Prussian forces at the Battle of Konitz. It was a tremendous clash in which both sides made heavy use of powerful crossbows—basically the medieval equivalent of the machine gun—to riddle each other with arrows. Once their arrows were expended, the rest of the fighting consisted mostly of up-close-and-personal hacking and slashing.

Initially, the Poles seemed to have the upper hand, overwhelming the Teutonic forces by sheer numerical superiority. But when the Polish army turned its attention to the Hussite wagons, which were heavily armored wagons laid out in a defensive formation, the knights' fortunes changed. These positions were heavily defended, and as the Polish forces charged, they were hit with a rain of arrows from rapid-fire crossbows, as well as a primitive form of cannon referred to as bombards. The Polish soldiers proved themselves altogether unprepared for this concentrated onslaught, and as numerous members of their company were struck down, the Teutonic Knights were able to rally their forces.

The conflict grew chaotic and disorderly as the Teutonic Knights tore into the Poles' undefended flanks. The enemy was forced to flee, and the Teutonic Knights were able to retake their lost territory. In all, it is said that Poland lost some 3,000 knights in this disaster, and another 339 were taken prisoner. It was most certainly a disaster for the Poles, but Polish King Casimir tried to recoup from these losses by hiring mercenaries of his own. He posted these hired warriors around Pomerania and Culmer Land (also called Chelmo Land or Culm) in order to prevent the Teutonic Knights from making any further inroads against them.

Soon, there was a standoff in the works that morphed into a full-blown stalemate between both sides. A quite staggering stalemate, as it would last until the signing of the Second Peace of Thorn on October 10th, 1466. With the signing of this agreement, the Teutonic Knights lost even more territory, as they had to hand over Western Prussia, which turned itself into an independent province of Poland. Poland was also granted access to Danzig, enabling the Poles an easy commute to the Baltic region.

Grand Master Ludwig von Erlichshausen would pass away the following year, and Heinrich Reuss von Plauen would be elected in his place. Heinrich Reuss von Plauen was distantly related to former Grand Master Heinrich von Plauen. His rule was a short one. He was most remembered for meeting with Polish King Casimir and making an oath to maintain peaceful relations while obstinately refusing to bow down to the king. Heinrich insisted the Teutonic Knights only reserved such an honor for the "pope and emperor."

If the Polish king was the superstitious type, he just might have convinced himself that this grand master's actions had consequences. On Heinrich's ride back from his meeting with Casimir, the grand master suffered a massive stroke. Coincidences like this happen all of the time, but for his opponents and perhaps even some of his allies, it must have seemed as if he was literally struck down from on high.

Grand Master Heinrich Reuss von Plauen would linger on in some capacity before perishing on January 2nd, 1470. Interestingly enough, the very next grand master of the Teutonic Order—Heinrich Reffle von Richtenberg—made sure that paying homage to the Polish king was the very first thing he did upon becoming the grand master.

One could speculate that perhaps Heinrich was indeed the superstitious type and sought to avoid the fate of his predecessor by humbling himself before Poland's king. Or, on the other hand, perhaps he was just less of an idealist and more of a pragmatist, knowing that such forced humility would serve the long-term objectives of the order.

Nevertheless, Grand Master Heinrich Reffle von Richtenberg would not have any easier of a time holding the shrinking dominion of the Teutonic Knights together. Little more is known of Grand Master Richtenberg since the declining order no longer kept its once meticulous records. Richtenberg himself passed away in 1477. He was remembered as a hard-working grand master who tirelessly sought to balance the order's budget by, among other things, keeping close track of expenses and gained revenue.

This grand master was succeeded by Martin Truchsess von Wetzhausen in August of 1477. Martin was a proud man who ended up becoming quite humble. When he first became grand master, he broke with the previous tradition and refused to bow down to the Polish king. King Casimir IV was willing to go to war for this offense, and the hostilities that followed were so devastating that by the summer of 1479, a defeated and much more meek Grand Master Martin Truchsess von Wetzhausen bowed to the Polish king.

The grand master and the Teutonic Order in general were rather low-key in the following years, with Wetzhausen primarily tending to domestic issues. The grand master's health then began to fail him, and he passed away quietly while resting at his residence in Konigsberg. His successor, Johann von Tiefen, did not want to repeat the mistakes of the last administration. He made sure to meet with the Polish king as soon as he was elected. By affirming his desire to be at peace with Poland, Grand Master Tiefen was better able to work on strengthening the ailing institution of the Teutonic Knights.

During Grand Master Johann von Tiefen's time as the leader of the Teutonic Knights, Polish King Casimir IV died. He was replaced by King John I Albert in 1492. Yes, that same year that Christopher Columbus sailed the ocean blue and a new world in America was discovered, Poland saw a new king step on the throne. The world was indeed at a crossroads, and as Europeans were stepping foot into the Americas, the Ottoman Turks were pushing deeper and deeper into Europe.

Constantinople had fallen decades before. This was the event that actually triggered the discovery of the Americas in the first place. The need for a water route to the East (the land route being blocked by the Turks at Constantinople) sent Columbus and other navigators sailing the oceans. And once Constantinople and the Balkans were in the Turks' grasp, they were not content to consolidate their gains. They pushed into Hungary and even began to threaten Austria and Poland.

For a group of crusading warriors like the Teutonic Knights, it seemed that their services just might once again be in demand. Polish King John I Albert, shortly after his coronation in 1492, called upon the knights to assemble themselves on the front lines along the shores of the Black Sea in an attempt to halt the Turkish advance. Grand Master Tiefen answered this call in 1497 and sent a few hundred knights to strategic points along the Black Sea.

However, their operations were interrupted when an epidemic broke out among the knights. Grand Master Tiefen himself ended up coming down with a bad case of dysentery. This illness caused him to hastily make an exit from the battlefield and head to the safety of the city of Lemberg (now the city of Lviv in modern-day Ukraine). He perished in Lemberg, and his mortal remains were interred at Konigsberg.

After Tiefen's death in 1497, he was succeeded by Grand Master Frederick (Friedrich) von Sachsen. Grand Master Frederick would be privileged to oversee yet another few years of the order's slow decline. During his reign, the brother organization of the Livonian Knights would see some hard fighting on the eastern front against the Russians. But after what seemed to be insurmountable odds, the Livonian Brothers of the Sword overcame even the might of Russian Tsar Ivan the Great, defeating the Russians at the Battle of Pskov in 1500.

Although the Teutonic Knights were not directly involved, this was a definite morale booster for the Teutonic Order. The rest of Frederick's time as the grand master would pass without much incident until his death in 1510. In truth, the Teutonic Order had been playing defense ever since the Battle of Tannenberg. But the next Teutonic knight in line to be grand master would change everything.

Chapter 8 – On A Tidal Wave of Teutonic Reformation

"Some tribes [of monkeys] have taken to washing potatoes in the river before eating them, others have not. Sometimes migrating groups of potato-washers meet non-washers, and the two groups watch each other's strange behavior with apparent bewilderment. But unlike the inhabitants of Lilliput who fought holy crusades over the question at which end to break the egg, the potato-washing monkeys do not go to war with the non-washers, because the poor creatures have no language which would enable them to declare washing a divine commandment and eating unwashed potatoes a deadly heresy."

-Arthur Koestler

Upon the death of Grand Master Frederick, many in the knighthood wished to move in a completely different direction. Tired of all of the mistakes of the past, the knights felt that radical reform was necessary in order to prevent a complete collapse of the Teutonic Order. The problem of repeated hostilities with Poland was an ever-present possibility, as always. Some in the order actually thought that perhaps they had found a solution to this problem by proposing to invite the king of Poland himself to become the grand master of the Teutonic Order.

The fact that they would even consider such a thing, something that would have been utterly abhorrent to their forebearers, shows just how far the knights had fallen. For those who were still horrified at the prospect, it turns out that they did not have much reason to worry. Polish King Sigismund I the Old was interested in the proposal, but at the end of the day, he could not stomach the vow of chastity that a grand master must take.

Nevertheless, the Teutonic Order soon elected their new grand master—Albrecht (sometimes anglicized to Albert) von Ansbach. Even though they could not convert the Polish king into a Teutonic Knight, they no doubt felt that they had the next best thing, for the young, twenty-year-old Albrecht was a man with connections. Not only was he a relative of the Polish king, but he was also kinfolk to the king of Hungary and Bohemia. On top of this, he was also closely connected to other important figures in the Holy Roman Empire and the Vatican. Yes, this young man was most certainly an insider, and it was hoped that all of these tight connections would help navigate the Teutonic Knights through their later years.

From the beginning, Albrecht grew his relationship with the Holy Roman emperor and became a regular attendee of the Imperial Diet. At Nuremberg in 1512, Albrecht discussed his dilemma with the Polish king. Prior to swearing allegiance to Holy Roman Emperor Maximillian I, Albrecht told him that it was necessary that he be liberated from having to bow down to the king of Poland—both figuratively and literally. The grand master was obviously attempting his hand at power politics by using the influence of one great power against another.

But the greatest power play of all would come from a most unexpected source. On October 31st, 1517, a German monk by the name of Martin Luther nailed his *Ninety-five Theses* to the door of Castle Church (sometimes called All Saints' Church) in Wittenberg. These theses were essentially complaints about the Catholic Church, as Luther felt the church was in desperate need of reform.

Luther found trouble with church policy in a wide range of areas, but most notable was his complaint about the sale of indulgences. Back then, the Catholic Church had a practice of granting an "indulgence" or absolution of sin for those willing to donate money for church causes. The paying of alms, of course, had been common from the beginning of the church, but Luther found the idea that the pope or anyone else could absolve one's sin simply by donating money absurd.

Most Christians today (at least Protestant Christians) would argue that only Jesus can forgive one's sins, but the Catholics had a different take. And contrary to popular opinion, it was not something they just made up—their views did indeed have some scriptural basis. The Catholic belief that the pope had the power to forgive sins, for example, stemmed from a verse in Mathew, in which Jesus tells Peter, whom the Catholics view as the first leader of the church (in other words, the pope), that whatever he "binds on earth" will be "bound in heaven."

Just to be clear, the exact scripture is from Mathew 18:18 and reads, "Truly I tell you, whatever you bind on Earth will be bound in heaven, and whatever you loose on Earth will be loosed in Heaven." It was actually from this verse that all sense of papal power was derived. The Catholics believed that the pope was God's vicar on Earth, and the seat of the papacy inherited from Peter continued to live by this motto—that the pope was specifically given the power to "bind and loose" people of their sins.

Catholics and Protestants can argue all day long on this point, but what Martin Luther found even more repugnant than a pope accepting indulgences and granting absolution in order to fund the church was the idea that the pope could even forgive the sins of the dead, shortening their time in purgatory. This practice was indeed quite common in Luther's day. The relatives of a deceased loved one would naturally be worried about the state of their dearly departed, so they would often pay alms on their behalf and bid the pope pray that any stay in purgatory would be a brief one.

The church always needed funding to build churches, to give to widows and orphans, or to launch future Crusades. And church officials knew that the granting of indulgences was quite lucrative. There was a demand for prayers for the souls of the deceased, and the church was willing to supply it in exchange for almsgiving.

A contemporary of Martin Luther, a Dominican friar named Johann Tetzel, famously capitalized on this very sentiment. He even went as far as to develop a rather catchy jingle to attract customers. He would go around villages with his money box, cheerfully announcing, "As soon as a coin in the coffer rings/The soul from purgatory springs!" Martin Luther was disgusted by this unbridled marketing and felt it was unbiblical.

Most Protestants today would tell you there is nothing at all scriptural about indulgences and praying for the dead. But that is actually not true. If anyone questioned the practice, Catholics would point to the Book of the Maccabees (a book Martin Luther conveniently tossed out of subsequent Protestant Bibles). In the Book of the Maccabees, we have the story of Judas Maccabeus telling his subjects to offer alms for the souls of slain soldiers so that the dead men's sins could be forgiven.

Another can of worms to open in regard to Catholics and Protestants is the whole concept of there being a purgatory—an in-between waiting place for souls—between heaven and hell. Although Protestants deny its existence, the Catholic Church's belief in purgatory stems from the biblical concept of "Sheol," sometimes called "paradise," where the Old Testament saints who were unable to get into heaven are said to have gone prior to the crucifixion (and atonement) of Jesus Christ. In the Greek New Testament, references to Sheol were often translated as Hades.

Although later Protestant translators often confused Hades and hell, these are two very different destinations. Hades is not hell. Hades is the Greek word for the underworld of the dead and was therefore viewed by the writers of the New Testament as a suitable equivalent of the Jewish word Sheol. While hell is a place of torment, Hades is a neutral location where the dead simply wait for judgment. Hades/Sheol, therefore, is purgatory.

Martin Luther never really disavowed his belief in purgatory, but he certainly had trouble with the concept, especially as it pertained to the idea that almsgiving could "spring a soul" from purgatory. It was with these doubts and concerns in mind that Luther nailed his written complaints to the doors of the church.

Whether you agree with Martin Luther's criticism of the Catholic Church or not, you have to admit that he was a rather bold and courageous individual. Martin Luther was a very brave man for even daring to question the Vatican since the last priest who really tried—Jan Hus—was burned at the stake for heresy. But the times were changing, and the power of German princes and nobles, in particular, had long been breaking from the Vatican.

And Martin Luther would fully take advantage of the growing German nationalistic sentiment, as the Germans were more likely to view papal decrees from Rome as troublesome foreign intrusions rather than actually taking them seriously. As Martin Luther's views made the rounds, the young grand master of the Teutonic Knights, Albrecht von Ansbach, could not help but perk up his ears.

By the time of Albrecht's visit to Nuremberg in 1522, according to writer and Teutonic scholar William Urban, "it was clear that he had been visibly affected by Lutheran teachings." Also present at the Diet of Nuremberg in 1522 was Andreas Osiander, who was himself a Catholic priest turned budding Protestant. The grand master and Andreas would form a close relationship as the grand master's ideas on Protestantism continued to evolve.

The following year, Martin Luther began to openly court the Teutonic Knights by issuing an argument against what he referred to as the "false chastity" that had been imposed upon the Teutonic Order. At one point, Martin Luther even wrote exclusively on behalf of the knights in regard to this very topic.

In his writings, Martin proclaimed, "Marvel not, dear Knights of the Teutonic Order, that I have made bold to address to you a special writing, and to advise you to give up your unchaste chastity and to marry. My intentions are altogether good. Besides, many sincere and intelligent men regard it as not merely helpful, but even necessary, to look to you to do this, because your order is indeed a unique order, differing from others most of all in that it was founded for the purpose of making war against infidels. It must therefore wield the worldly sword and be a secular order at the same time that it is to be a spiritual order and make and keep the vows of chastity, poverty and obedience like other monks. How that combination works, daily experience and reason teach us only too well."

Luther then went on to say, "Secondly, scarcely anyone will doubt that the Teutonic Order would in that case be less burdensome and more acceptable to all its subjects than it is at present. For it is notorious that as things are now, neither God nor the world derives much benefit from it. Besides, the knights are suspected and disliked because everyone knows how rare chastity is, and every man must be afraid for his wife and daughter. For they who are not married cannot be trusted very far, since even they that are married must be constantly on their guard lest they fall, although among them there is more justification for hope and confidence. Among the unmarried there is neither hope nor confidence, but only constant fear."

Here, Martin Luther clearly sought to tap into the German nationalism of the Teutonic Knights, as well as their discontent with the status quo. Martin Luther points out the contradiction of them using the worldly sword in battle yet not being allowed to marry, settle down, and have a family. He knew that although the knights did indeed remain single, very few were chaste. On the contrary, most sought relations outside of marriage, therefore operating under an "unchaste chastity." It was a painful façade that many knights had been forced to portray. But now, Martin Luther was offering the Teutonic Order a different path to take, if they would just accept it.

Grand Master Albrecht von Ansbach secretly met with Martin Luther in late 1523. During the meeting, the monk advised the grand master to discard his previous vows. Martin Luther instructed Albrecht to cast off his archaic vows of chastity and get married, start a family, and allow the previously monastic state of the Teutonic Order to become a secular one. All of these things must have been music to Grand Master Albrecht's ears, but just like many of his predecessors, he was a pragmatist at heart. And he was most certainly not ready to face the fallout of breaking with the church outright.

As such, even as Albrecht was entertaining these ideas, he was telling a completely different version of events to Pope Adrian VI. The grand master actually informed the pontiff that he was eager to "punish" members of the Teutonic Order who dared to become part of the Protestant movement. Nevertheless, as Martin Luther spread his teachings in German lands, including the Teutonic Knights' backyard of Prussia, they did not lift a finger to stop him. And as the popularity of Lutheranism grew, the knights were becoming ever-more confident that they would be able to break with the Catholic Church.

In the meantime, Albrecht was getting ample encouragement from the local nobility who wished to see the monastic state secularized, as well as from the king of Poland, who anticipated Prussia becoming a part of the Polish-Lithuanian Commonwealth. The fact that staunchly Catholic Poland would welcome a Protestant-leaning Prussia might seem more than a little odd, but the reasons were much more political than ideological. Poland became supportive of the transformation of Prussia into a secularized Protestant state as a means of striking out against the Holy Roman Empire and distancing Prussia from its influence.

As it pertains to the grand master of the Teutonic Knights, Albrecht saw a break from the church as the only logical means of ending the constant struggle with the Poles, which finally pushed him to act. On April 10th, 1525, Albrecht disavowed himself from his previous oaths, and with the blessing of Poland's king, he remade Prussia into a secular duchy. As a result, Albrecht became a duke.

And if all this was not enough, the following year, in 1526, he took the fateful step of marrying a Danish princess—Dorothea of Denmark. Dorothea's father, Frederick I, was one of the earliest Protestant rulers, and his backing was yet another reassurance for Grand Master Albrecht (now Duke Albrecht). Since the Teutonic Order's grand master was now a duke, they needed a new leader.

The Catholic Church, of course, was incensed over what had transpired, but there was not much it could do about it. Former Grand Master Albrecht was excommunicated, but unlike Jan Hus, who was burned at the stake, the long arm of the Vatican was unable to reach Grand Master Albrecht.

In the aftermath of this seismic shift, Walter von Cronberg was elected as the new grand master. However, the election of Walter von Cronberg was disputed by the grand master of the Livonian Knights, who felt that he was well positioned to be placed in the role instead. It seemed as if things were about to get ugly, but Holy Roman Emperor Charles V was able to mediate an agreement between the Livonian and Teutonic Orders in 1527. Consequently enough, it would be the Livonian branch of the Teutonic Knights that would soon be on the front lines.

Chapter 9 – On Battlefields Far and Wide

"When people talk as if the Crusades were nothing more than an aggressive raid against Islam, they seem to forget in the strangest way that Islam itself was only an aggressive raid against the old and ordered civilizations in these parts. I do not say it in mere hostility to the religion of Mahomet; I am fully conscious of many values and virtues in it; but certainly it was Islam that was the invasion and Christendom that was the thing invaded."

-Gilbert K. Chesterton

By the 1540s, the landscape of Eastern Europe had changed considerably. Lithuania was no longer pagan. Poland was a strong nation state, and the Holy Roman Empire was in decline. The Ottoman Empire, in the meantime, was still on the rise, and so was the realm of the Rus or, as it would later be known, Russia.

Ever since the fall of Constantinople in 1453, Russian monarchs viewed themselves as the inheritors of not just the Eastern Orthodox faith, which they espoused, but also the imperial power of the Byzantine Empire. It was for this reason that Russian kings began to be referred to as tsars, which was a Russian variation of the old Roman term "Caesar." In 1547, one of the most infamous tsars of all,

Ivan IV—perhaps better known as Ivan the Terrible—would rise to prominence. Ivan spent much of his reign tackling the Tartars and the vestiges of the Mongolian horde that had once threatened all of Russia. Once the Russian East was won, Ivan the Terrible began to look toward his western borders and the realm of the Livonian Knights.

Ivan IV's grandfather, Ivan III (also known as Ivan the Great), had already tangled with the knights in 1500 and was defeated. But by the time of Ivan the Terrible, the Russians had grown considerably in strength while the Teutonic Knights—the Livonian Order included—had grown weaker. The notion that Russia could gain Livonia, which comprised modern-day Estonia and Latvia, in one fell swoop was just too tempting for Ivan IV to ignore. So, in 1557/1558, Ivan the Terrible unleashed his troops on Livonian lands.

At the outset, the Livonian Knights appeared to be completely overwhelmed and were forced back on their heels. Many of the knights' own subjects also openly rebelled, and some ran to the Russians with open arms, viewing them as "liberators" from the sometimes harsh and austere rule of the German knights. The Livonian Knights were able to rally, however, and in 1560, they finally pushed the Russians back when the two armies collided near the Teutonic settlement of Revel (sometimes spelled Reval). It was at this point that the powers of Poland, Sweden, and Denmark all decided to intervene. Although they all sided with the Livonian Knights, some certainly had their own ulterior motives, perhaps seeking to carve out territory for themselves in the Baltic.

At any rate, all of them were against the Russians, and after the Russians were pushed back, both sides dug in place. A bloody stalemate would ensue, which would continue over the next several years. The stalemate was finally broken in 1578 when the Livonian Knights and their allies were able to deal the Russians such a heavy blow that they were practically knocked out of the war.

Intermittent skirmishes would continue, but Ivan the Terrible knew that he had lost. After a few years of stalled negotiations, he managed to get the pope to mediate a lasting truce in 1583.

The Livonian Order, in the meantime, had essentially been dissolved, and it agreed to hand over Livonia to Polish authority. This meant that the Duchy of Prussia, with Konigsberg as its capital, was the only remaining territory in the hands of the Teutonic Knights. This piece of real estate would remain in Teutonic hands until it was handed over to the powerful dynasty of the Hohenzollerns in 1618, who served as electors for the Holy Roman Empire.

When the former Teutonic grand master turned Prussian duke Albrecht died in 1568, he passed the administration of the duchy to his own son, Albrecht Friedrich (Albert Frederick). However, Albrecht Friedrich was a troubled soul, and after a mental breakdown, Elector Joachim Frederick of Brandenburg was appointed to serve as the ailing Albrecht Friedrich's regent in 1605. (Electors were the men who served as part of the election process of the Holy Roman emperor.)

Joachim himself is an interesting character. He was a Catholic, but he was open to Protestant ideas and did not stifle the Protestant leanings of others. He was also an elector, which gave him considerable influence over the Holy Roman Empire. Whether the candidate for Holy Roman emperor was Catholic, Protestant, or an amalgamation of both, they would have certainly courted this elector's vote. And the same could be said for the Hohenzollerns, who were ultimately handed the duchy in 1618.

This put the Duchy of Prussia in an interesting position of having both Poland and the Holy Roman Empire vying for its favor. Prussia was suddenly a small land that could wield considerable influence. At any rate, as it pertains to the Teutonic Knights, the stateless order, although reduced in power, would come into the employ of a branch of the Austro-Hungarian military called the "Hoch und

Deutschmeister." Along with this, the knights would also be recruited for various sporadic conflicts in the region over the next several years.

In 1683, for example, the Teutonic Knights played a role—albeit a small one—in the defense of Vienna when the Ottoman Empire besieged Austria. The Teutonic Knights were directed by Grand Master Ludwig Anton von Pfalz-Neuburg, while the Ottoman march on Austria was led by the Turkish Grand Vizier Kara Mustafa Pasha. The grand vizier had meticulously planned the invasion, and he worked hard to build up a formidable army. This great force surrounded Vienna and repeatedly hammered away at the city's walled fortifications as the outnumbered defenders inside braced for impact.

The walls were strong, however, so the Turks began to have their engineers dig tunnels under the walls so that they could put explosive mines in place. Once detonated, the walls would come crashing down. But thanks to vigilant defenders, who would charge into a tunnel, kill the miners, and disable the explosives, the Ottomans' repeated attempts were foiled. All the same, the Austrians were waging a losing battle, and it was just a matter of time before Vienna, like Constantinople and so many other former Christian lands, would fall into Ottoman hands.

But unlike Constantinople, where there was no last-minute respite or quarter, right when it seemed that Vienna was about to be overrun, an army of Christian knights appeared on the western horizon. These knights were led by the Polish king himself—Jan (John) III Sobieski. His forces consisted primarily of the Polish brand of Crusaders: the Winged Hussars.

The Winged Hussars were entirely formidable in their own right. Just as the name implies, these knights had wings on their backs! Actually, it was a wooden frame attached to their armor, which they decorated with feathers. This created a spectacular sight. Imagine seeing these knights charging down on the enemy from atop their horses; they would appear as winged, sword-wielding avengers. The beleaguered citizens of Vienna were no doubt praying for angels to come down and rescue them—the Winged Hussars must have seemed like a close approximation of what they were asking for!

Besides the psychological impact these knights, who were essentially suited up like archangels, had, there was also a practical purpose behind the wings. The winged frame was useful in obscuring the knights from artillery fire, and it also protected them from sword strikes to their back since the sword would have to go through the wooden frame protruding from their shoulders first.

At any rate, along with these fearsome Winged Hussars, there was also a small contingent of Teutonic Knights in the mix. The idea of Poles and Teutons fighting side by side would have been unheard of in centuries past, but with their previous squabbles set to the side, these warriors fought for a common purpose—saving Vienna. They charged at the Turkish positions and rapidly cut through their ranks.

The Turks were not expecting this onslaught. And making matters worse, the sultan, rather than directing his main force on the Poles and their Teutonic allies, belligerently kept the demolition of Vienna's walls as his primary objective. However, as the Poles tore through the Turkish infantry, the sultan was soon forced to call for his troops to make a hasty retreat.

If it were not for the efforts of these crusading warriors, Vienna would have suffered the same fate as Constantinople, and history would have played out very differently. Not only would Vienna have become a Turkish-speaking hub of Islam, but the Turkish advance could also very well have pushed on to conquer the rest of Western Europe. The Teutonic Knights and their colleagues stood firm at the gates of Vienna, however, and made sure that the mighty Ottoman Empire advanced no farther. And as for the Ottomans, rather than continuing to conquer European land, their failure would mark the beginning of a long, slow decline. Soon, the once-feared Ottoman Empire would be dismissed as the "sick man of Europe."

The siege of Vienna was not just a terrific battle but also one of the greatest turning points in history. And it was one in which the Teutonic Knights themselves were able to take part. In 1697, the Teutonic Knights once again manned the field to take on the Ottoman Turks. The order joined forces with a European coalition led by the Habsburg Monarchy in the Battle of Zenta, which took place in Serbia.

The Battle of Zenta resulted from an Ottoman attempt to seize all of Hungary for itself. Although the defending coalition was outnumbered, they managed to deal a tremendous blow to the Ottomans, killing some thirty thousand of their number while the European coalition lost only a few hundred. The end result of this bitter defeat forced the Ottomans to sign the Treaty of Karlowitz, which placed Hungary, Croatia, Slavonia, and Transylvania under the jurisdiction of Austria.

It is rather interesting to note that the Teutonic Knights were on the scene when Transylvania was delivered from the Ottomans since this piece of Balkan territory had once served as a Teutonic base. The Battle of Zenta, in fact, would be the final major military operation of which the Teutonic Knights were a part. So, it seems almost fitting that these warriors apparently ended the crusading chapter of their service at one of the places where the Teutonic Order first took root.

Chapter 10 – The Later Years of the Teutonic Order

"The world calls for, and expects from us, simplicity of life, the spirit of prayer, charity towards all, especially towards the lowly and the poor, obedience and humility, detachment, and self-sacrifice. Without this mark of holiness, our word will have difficulty in touching the heart of modern man."

-Pope Paul VI

At the dawning of the 1700s, what remained of the Teutonic Order had become increasingly listless and largely without purpose. The next major crisis the Teutonic Order faced was when France erupted in tumult in 1789. French revolutionaries sought to topple not only the Ancien Régime ("Old Regime") of France but also many other aged institutions throughout Europe. It would not be long before what remained of the Teutonic Knights would be in their crosshairs as well.

Soon, Teutonic lands all along the Rhine were being confiscated by French revolutionaries. The French Revolution then coalesced around the French general-turned-dictator, Napoleon Bonaparte. Once Napoleon Bonaparte rose to the top after the French Revolution, he made it clear that he had no stomach for the orders of knights. First, he went after the Knights Hospitaller, overrunning their island base in Malta.

Shortly after dispatching the Knights Hospitaller on Malta, Napoleon turned his attention to the Teutonic Knights. He had any members of the Teutonic Order who found themselves under his dominion removed from their posts. Once Napoleon was through, all that remained of the Teutonic Order was the few holdings protected by the Austrian Crown that Napoleon had failed to seize. Nevertheless, Napoleon seemed prepared to utterly ignore this vestige, famously declaring on April 24th, 1809, "The Teutonic Order is abolished!"

Napoleonic France was ultimately bested by a powerful European coalition. For the most part, the vast majority of the Teutonic Knights would never have the lands that were confiscated from them fully restored. There were some exceptions, though. For instance, William Orange of the Netherlands returned territory in Holland to the Teutonic Knights in 1815. At any rate, whatever holdouts of the order remained, they would keep a low profile over the next few decades.

In 1839, at the behest of Ferdinand I of Austria, the Teutonic Knights were transformed into frontline medics to serve the Austrian army. Just as the knights had done at their inception in the Holy Land, they once again returned to the selfless task of fielding sickbed infirmaries. This role was then expanded in 1866 with the establishment of a chapter called Honorable Knights of the Teutonic Order. For these knights, volunteer work at hospitals was a requirement that needed to be fulfilled annually. In 1871, a female volunteer group dedicated to a similar service was established. However, it was in the First World War that the Teutonic Knights' efforts as field medics really shined.

Right at the outbreak of the war in 1914, the Teutonic Knights were busy tending to the thousands of sick, banged-up, bullet-wounded, and bludgeoned troops who were being pulled up from the trenches. It was certainly a noble calling. But one of the great ironies of the Teutonic Order's services during World War One was that they were actually fighting (at least in a euphemistic sense) on the side of the Ottoman Turks!

Yes, during the war, Austria was aligned with Germany, and Germany was aligned with Turkey. These Central Powers faced off against the Allied forces, which were led by Britain, France, Russia, and the United States. One could speculate that many a Teutonic grand master might have rolled over in their grave at the thought that their previous mortal enemy would be aligned with the Teutonic Order in the 20th century.

But times had most certainly changed. The Ottoman Empire had shrunk to a mere vestige of what it had formerly been, and its ideological wars of conquest were largely a thing of the past. Since the Ottoman Empire's days of decline had become entangled in European power politics, it was hedging its bets on one European power after another. By 1914, it just so happened that Germany (and therefore Austria) had interests that aligned with the Ottomans.

Showing just how deep memories can run in Europe, one of the earliest battles of the war, which happened to take place at Tannenberg, took on huge significance for the war's German-speaking participants. Tannenberg, you might recall, was the site of the famous defeat of Teutonic forces some five hundred years prior in 1410.

This time around, however, German troops were able to make short work of two large Russian regiments in August of 1914. Although this battle and World War One in general had nothing to do with the true legacy of the Teutonic Knights, excited German nationalists could not help but conflate the two together. And it was then presented by propagandists as somehow being a vindication of the Teutonic defeat of 1410.

The Central Powers, of course, would end up being defeated in 1918, and the subsequent Treaty of Versailles, which was signed on June 28th, 1919, would have consequences for all of those involved. First and foremost, as it pertains to the Teutonic Knights, was the collapse of the Austro-Hungarian Empire. Austria, Hungary, and all of the other components of the empire came unglued. This meant that the Teutonic Knights had lost their biggest benefactor. To be sure, they did still retain some support in Austria proper, but their resources and influence as an order were greatly diminished.

The Teutonic Knights had lost any real say in world affairs, yet in the aftermath of the Treaty of Versailles, they were often used as a tool of propaganda by others. The Marxists in Russia, which had turned to communism during the war, pointed to the Teutonic Knights as symbols of German belligerence. The Germans, on the other hand, still smarting from their bitter defeat in the war, began to paint the Teutonic Knights no longer as a Catholic military order but rather in purely nationalistic terms.

The Teutonic Knights were indeed used by German propagandists to not only make the general sense of German martial valor seem heroic but also justify the concept of creating a larger Germany based upon the Teutonic lands of old. The Nazis would use the former dominions of the Teutonic Knights as a blueprint for their so-called *Lebensraum* or, as it translates in English, "living space." After all, at their height, the Teutonic Knights had fortresses stretching from France to Ukraine, which were all lands that the Nazis would later storm through to claim as their own.

But as much as Nazi Germans would propagandize the history of the Teutonic Knights for their own ends, Hitler and his cronies actually hated what remained of the Teutonic Order, especially its Catholic ties. Hitler secretly despised Christianity. And much in line with this contempt, he naturally found a group with deep ties to the Catholic Church as highly suspect. Hitler saw the Teutonic Order as nothing more than the eyes and ears of the pope in his territory. The Nazis also despised groups they viewed as being too secretive with their own rituals and routines. And the Teutonic Knights was an exclusive club, so it was viewed very much like the Freemasons, who were also greatly persecuted.

So, due to Hitler's distaste of the Teutonic Order, one of the first things he did upon taking over Austria in 1938 was seize the knights' remaining land and abolish the last remnants of the order. So much for Nazi love of the Teutonic Knights! Rather than being admired, some members of the Teutonic Order eventually found themselves under arrest and held against their will. Even so, the despicable fascists continued to use the name and imagery of the order for their own ends.

Fortunately, Germany and its Axis partners were defeated. And although much damage had been done, a free and independent Austria was able to restore some of the lands and prestige of the Teutonic Order in 1947. There wasn't much left to the Teutonic Knights, but it was a fresh start all the same.

The revived Teutonic Order was able to resume its charity work, and it even expanded chapters outside of Austria, such as a pilgrim hostel that was put up in Rome in 1957, which worked in sync with the Teutonic Procurator General to the Holy See. This hostel specialized in aiding German-speaking visitors in Rome, such as those on pilgrimage to see sacred sites like, for example, St. Peter's Basilica."

Such efforts would seem to be a full return to the Teutonic Knights' original mission when they were first conceived as the Hospital of Saint Mary of the Germans in the Holy Land. Recall that at the Teutonic Order's inception, they served as a charitable organization aiding German-speaking pilgrims to the Levant. Now, once again, the inheritors of the order were serving much the same role.

And after opening its doors to more volunteers, the Catholic Church was able to reorganize the Teutonic Knights as a strictly religious order, a transition that Pope Paul VI made permanent in 1965. The Teutonic Order remains popular to this very day, with volunteers working on charitable and religious projects far and wide.

One of the oldest charitable chapters of the Teutonic Knights still in operation is in Holland. Bailiwick of Utrecht of the Teutonic Order is based out of Utrecht in the Netherlands. This organization specializes in caring for the sick, as well as giving aid to the homeless and providing recovery services for those dealing with substance abuse issues. The latter of which has become a very important form of modern-day outreach.

It is indeed a worthy cause, especially in the Netherlands, a country with a known history of drug addiction. This was highlighted by Holland's Minister of Justice and Security, Ferdinand Grapperhaus, who, in 2020, infamously proclaimed, "The Netherlands is at risk of becoming a narco state!" Likening the country's drug crisis to a nation that uses drugs as a marketable commodity may be a bit extreme. But the Netherlands has indeed become known for its wide range of recreational drug use, as well as its typically lax laws surrounding them. But for those trying to escape their addictions, the Bailiwick of Utrecht of the Teutonic Order is there for them.

The work of this charity is currently overseen by the group's so-called "Land Commander"–Jan Reint de Vos van Steenwijk. For Jan Reint de Vos Steenwijk and his fellow brethren of the Teutonic Order, every life saved is always well worth the effort. If they can be the knight in (figuratively) shining armor for those going through troubling and hard times, they are more than happy to don that armor and serve others to the best of their abilities. And the world is a better place for their efforts.

Conclusion: From the Crusades to Humanitarian Aid

"One aspect of neighborly love is that we must not merely will our neighbors good—but actually work to bring it about."

-Thomas Aquinas

The Teutonic Knights were forged in the battlefields of war. But at the outset, their objective was not so much to fight as to render aid. The Crusades, of course, were a bloody and horribly violent business, and as such, there was no shortage of wounded souls to which to tend.

The Teutonic Order was, at its inception, a predominantly German enterprise, with deep links to the Germanic-based Holy Roman Empire. These connections would help persuade the pope to sanction the expansion of the Teutonic Knights into a full-fledged fighting force. But it was not long before the Teutonic Knights were redirected from the main goal of the Crusaders'—retaking Jerusalem—and sent to do battle in Eastern Europe instead.

First, the Teutonic Knights were sent to fight the infidels in Transylvania, but when this later turned unfashionable in the minds of wary heads of state in the Balkans, the knights were sent farther north to shore up Christian expansion into the Baltic. Here, the Teutonic

Knights would join forces with the previous order of the Livonian Knights, and they would set down roots that would last several centuries.

The knights' main goal was to root out the last pagans of the Baltic, which they did with ruthless efficiency. But once this great task was complete, the order seemed to lose its ability to justify its purpose. And after increasing conflicts with Poland, as well as a fully converted Lithuania, the Teutonic Order was slowly chipped away at until it was a mere vestige of its former self.

By the 1500s, many in the Teutonic Order were desperately looking for change, and it was at this crossroads that the German monk Martin Luther's Reformation occurred. Luther developed a personal relationship with the Teutonic Knights and urged them to discard their "false chastity" for a more realistic position as a secular order.

Since the Teutonic Knights no longer had a primary objective and did indeed feel that they were perpetuating a façade on many levels, Martin Luther's entreaty certainly made a lot of sense. In fact, they related so much to Luther's words that the grand master of the knights would give up his vows to become a secular duke.

This was not the end of the monastic order, however, as variations of it would continue throughout the centuries. Even the likes of both Napoleon Bonaparte and Adolf Hitler could not fully disband the Teutonic Order; there would still be a vestige of the original Catholic order. And indeed, this Catholic order still persists to this day. Although the Teutonic Knights are no longer seen charging onto battlefields, their influence can be felt in charitable work all around the globe.

Considering the fact that it was through selfless acts of charity that the knights began their work, it is indeed fitting that they have come full circle in this regard. From the Crusades to humanitarian aid, the Teutonic Knights have fulfilled their purpose, and they have fulfilled it well. But that does not mean that they were always above reproach.

During the Teutonic Order's existence, they have most certainly committed their fair share of misdeeds. They were brutal in their forced conversion of pagans in Eastern Europe, and even once the pagans converted, the knights often proved themselves to be harsh taskmasters to those converts living under their dominion.

At times, the grand masters of the Teutonic Order presented themselves more as greedy opportunists than the heralds of the higher cause that they were meant to proclaim. There is certainly much criticism that can be made when one considers the entirety of the order's existence. But there is no doubt that the Teutonic Knights were among the most long-lived initiatives sparked by the Crusades.

Here's another book by Captivating History that you might like

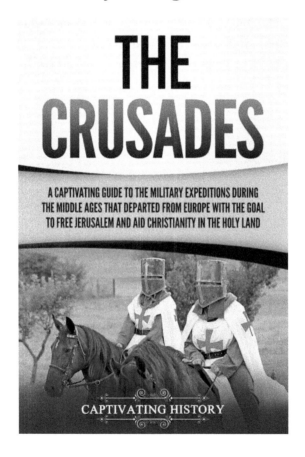

Free Bonus from Captivating History (Available for a Limited time)

Hi History Lovers!

Now you have a chance to join our exclusive history list so you can get your first history ebook for free as well as discounts and a potential to get more history books for free! Simply visit the link below to join.

Captivatinghistory.com/ebook

Also, make sure to follow us on Facebook, Twitter and Youtube by searching for Captivating History.

Ingram Content Group UK Ltd.
Milton Keynes UK
UKHW021954100323
418410UK00006B/220